The Place Value Connection

**Primary Activities and Games to Teach
Place Value, Money, and More**

Diana A. D'Aboy

DALE SEYMOUR PUBLICATIONS

Cover design: Deborah Hopping
Illustrations: Rachel Gage, Bill Eral, Diana D'Aboy

Order number DS01521
ISBN 0-86651-269-1

DALE
SEYMOUR
PUBLICATIONS
P.O. BOX 10888
PALO ALTO, CA 94303

defghi-MA-8932109

Acknowledgments

I wish to thank Carol LeDuc, my math assistant, for suggesting a pictorial 1 to 100 chart so students can see our numeration system as a whole. That suggestion initiated the development of the charts and the activities in this book. I thank her for the many delightful hours we worked together to develop and experiment with activities and teaching strategies.

I also want to thank Chris Druffel, my other math assistant, for her help in creating the materials and for her continual encouragement. I am grateful as well to my colleagues who requested that I publish the charts, which encouraged me to complete this endeavor.

Holly Wunder did the careful editorial work, and Beverly Cory guided the manuscript through production. I am indeed grateful to them and to Dale Seymour for their support and help throughout this project.

Special thanks to my husband, John E. D'Aboy, for his patient and loving endorsement and his proofreading throughout the time I was writing this book. He and our four children have always inspired me to develop my skills. They have also asked perceptive questions that have helped me to refine the concepts and activities presented in this book.

Contents

Introduction

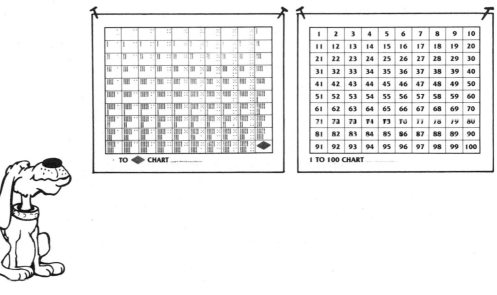

Student teachers, first-year teachers, and experienced teachers alike always welcome new and better ways to help children learn mathematical concepts. *The Place Value Connection*, developed from the author's own teaching experience, is intended to meet that need.

The Place Value Connection is based on the use of the familiar hundreds chart as a small, clearly defined universe in which primary children can work and play to develop their mathematical skills. Special pictorial and numeral 1 to 100 charts may be purchased from Dale Seymour Publications for use with this book. These charts were designed to help students visualize our numeration system and see it as a whole. Through repeated use of both charts, their visual image becomes a referent in the child's mind for understanding many mathematical concepts.

This book gives you more than 100 activities for teaching place value and related mathematical concepts to children in the primary grades. Many of the activities use the 1 to 100 charts; others incorporate a variety of familiar manipulatives—base ten blocks, bean sticks, multilinks. The goal is to combine the *concrete*, the *pictorial*, and the *abstract* for an active, holistic learning experience.

The book is divided into seven parts, as follows:

- Part 1 discusses the educational philosophy of the charts.
- Part 2 describes materials used in the various activities.
- Part 3 presents prerequisite activites for primary teachers to do with their students prior to using the charts. You can choose how many activities are appropriate for your class as well as to what depth your students need to experience each activity.

- Part 4 presents activities for teaching place value using the charts.
- Part 5 presents activities for addition and subtraction.
- Part 6 presents activities for multiplication and division.
- Part 7 emphasizes teaching money concepts using cut-outs, play money, and the 1 to 100 charts.

At the back of this book are 39 reproducible pages you may duplicate for classroom use with the listed activities. These include small, individual student versions of the pictorial and numeral charts, a similar blank chart, 3 × 3 and 5 × 2 grids, flash cards, expanded notation cards, sign circles, a place value mat, a tens and ones mat, an addition and subtraction mat, a fair trade mat, a money mat, four sets of double spinners for naming numbers, more or less and money spinners, coin cut-outs, and worksheets.

As you use these activities, your mode of teaching will shift from working with the whole class for teaching a concept, to working with small groups for better understanding, to providing individuals with experiences at learning centers for reinforcement. You can respond to students' needs by furnishing good learning materials and by organizing the classroom for efficient group and individual learning. Because the learning activities in this book are for the whole class, small math groups, or individuals at learning centers, they are readily adaptable to varied teaching and learning styles. Visual, auditory, and kinesthetic styles of learning are incorporated into the activites. When *Active* appears after the title of an activity, students will use whole body movements. The activities are not arranged in an exact sequential order because many of them are closely linked, even mutually dependent; however, the general order progresses from easier to more difficult.

Educational Philosophy

Mathematics involves the search for patterns and relationships that are not always obvious. As students see and discriminate among patterns, they are using a powerful tool for exploring number concepts and mathematical relationships. The 1 to 100 charts and the activities in this book will help students develop the ability to see patterns, to understand place value and our numeration and monetary systems, and to use problem-solving strategies.

Children learn best when they can work with manipulative materials prior to being exposed to pictures or abstract symbols. A strong visual representation of the manipulatives provides an important link to the abstract symbols. Thus these charts are best used after students have had some experience with manipulatives such as base ten blocks, bean sticks, ten-frames, or multilinks. The 1 to 100 *pictorial* chart provides visual pictures of tens and ones, and the 1 to 100 *numeral* chart illustrates the abstract symbols that make up our numeration system.

When using base ten blocks, students accumulate 10 ones and then trade or regroup them into a set of ten. This trading is illustrated by the flaps; 10 ones become a set of ten (sometimes referred to as a *ten stick*), repeatedly, until 10 tens become a set of 100. The two names for those numbers are shown pictorially.

For example, 30 is shown as 2 tens and 10 ones, and on the flap it is shown as 3 tens. "Trading in" becomes a useful referent for the student when learning regrouping in addition and subtraction at a later time.

The Pictorial Chart

There are several reasons for the arrangement of the ones and tens on the pictorial chart. Because the human eye can take in only five objects in a random arrangement without some grouping, there are never more than 5 ones or 5 tens grouped together on the chart. Also notice that as the ones increase by one more in each square as you move across a row to the right, they do not change their previous position in space. This shows visually the "one more" concept of our numeration system. The numbers greater than 5 can be identified as "5 plus some more." Children can learn to count on from 5 until they have two 5's to make a 10. This makes counting by fives just as easy as counting by tens. This is particularly helpful for teaching students to count money, because they count on from a nickel until they have two nickels to trade for a dime.

This kind of visual imagery can help students learn addition facts as well. For example, when an addition problem has two addends that are 5 or greater, it can be reduced to a question of 10 + ? = ? as shown below.

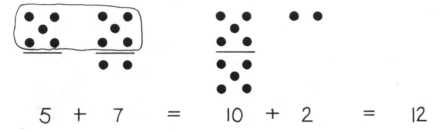

The "5 plus some more" is also a helpful configuration for understanding rounding to the nearest ten.

Teaching the Numbers 11 to 19

We encourage students to use nicknames for the numbers from 11 to 19, because their real names are illogical when considered with the rest of the names in our numeration system. When other numbers are read from left to right, we can write what we hear ("twenty-three," 23). But "thir-teen," for example, sounds like "three-teen," so students often write it as 31. Thus we suggest using the real names *and* the nicknames for the numbers from 11 to 19: eleven and "onety-one," twelve and "onety-two," thirteen and "onety-three," and so on. If you are not comfortable using these names, skip the numbers from 11 to 19 when teaching the meaning of tens and ones. After students have learned the meaning of the numbers from 20 to 99, return to the teen row and help students understand why it is hard.

Copy the number-names chart (figure 1) on the chalkboard to help students learn to read and understand these names. Highlight the TEEN and TY with two bright colors.

0	zero					
1	one	11	eleven	or "oneTY-one"	10	oneTY (ten)
2	two	12	twelve	or "oneTY-two"	20	twenTY
3	three	13	thirTEEN	or "oneTY-three"	30	thirTY
4	four	14	fourTEEN	or "oneTY-four"	40	forTY
5	five	15	fifTEEN	or "oneTY-five"	50	fifTY
6	six	16	sixTEEN	or "oneTY-six"	60	sixTY
7	seven	17	sevenTEEN	or "oneTY-seven"	70	sevenTY
8	eight	18	eighTEEN	or "oneTY-eight"	80	eighTY
9	nine	19	nineTEEN	or "oneTY-nine"	90	nineTY
10	ten					

Figure 1.   **Understanding Number Names**

4

Summary
When we provide students with a broad base of experience and allow plenty of time for them, they can assimilate mathematical concepts into their mental structures. A teacher's first priority is to nurture and facilitate that process. When we provide a wide variety of experiences, strong tools for learning, and the gift of time, we give students the power to learn for themselves. We hope you will enjoy using the 1 to 100 charts and the activities in this book to help students feel at ease with the world of mathematics.

"TELL ME, I FORGET;
SHOW ME, I REMEMBER;
INVOLVE ME, I UNDERSTAND."

Materials

Many different types of activities are presented in Parts 3 through 7 of this book. Part 2 makes suggestions for preparing the charts and manipulative materials that are recommended in these activities. The materials you will need with any given activity are listed with the activity itself, but you will have to refer to these pages for the details on making or preparing the needed items.

Keep in mind that if you duplicate the reproducible pages at the back of this book on cardstock and then laminate them, you can use the same ones in the classroom year after year. Other materials, such as the beansticks, should be made anew with the students each year. The instructions for preparing needed materials follow.

1. THE 1 TO 100 CHARTS. These two charts—one pictorial, one with numerals to 100—can be purchased as a set (Dale Seymour Publications, order number DS01520). Laminate these large charts to extend their life. Cut on all the dotted lines on the right-hand side of the large *pictorial* chart. Then fold all the flaps toward the face of the chart. Crease the flaps so they will be flat when folded.

You will need one set of the charts for bulletin board display. You may want to order additional sets of charts to use in making these materials:

Number line strips. Cut each of the two charts into horizontal, 10 × 1 strips.

Numeral and pictorial cards. On the numeral chart, underline the numbers 6, 9, 16, 18, 19, 61, 66, 68, 69, 81, 86, 89, 91, 96, 98, and 99. (This will prevent reading any numbers upside down after they are cut apart.) Then cut both the pictorial and numeral charts into squares to make two decks of 100 cards each.

Poke-and-peek cards. These are especially valuable for individual student use at learning centers. Make these cards as follows: Cut apart two large charts to make two decks of individual cards. On the pictorial cards, write three numerals as possible answers (two wrong and one correct). Use a paper punch to make holes above each numeral, and then circle the correct hole on the back of the card. This makes each card self-correcting. On the numeral cards, write *even* and *odd,* punch holes above the words, and once again circle the correct hole on the back of the card.

EXAMPLES:

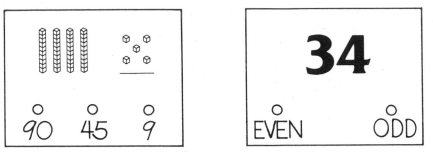

2. **CARD RACKS.** Make some card racks to use with the cards made from the large pictorial and numeral charts. Cut a long one-by-two-inch board into 18" lengths and cut a slot down the middle to hold the cards. Young children have difficulty holding many cards in their hands, so these racks are handy. An inverted egg carton also makes a good card rack.

3. **BLANK CHARTS.** Make and laminate several large 10 × 10 blank charts on railroad board. Make them the same size as the large pictorial and numeral charts.

4. **NUMBER FRAMES.** Make a *catcher's mitt* and a *window pane frame* for framing numbers on the large charts. Make the catcher's mitt from brown railroad board, cutting a 2" × 3" rectangle out of the middle and attaching a ruler as the handle. To make the window pane frame, draw twenty-five 2" × 3" window panes on poster board in a five-by-five grid. Then cut out the center window pane.

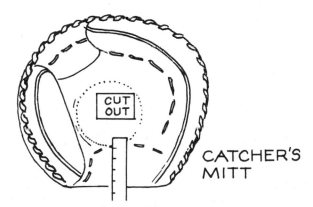

CATCHER'S MITT   WINDOW PANE FRAME

5. **TRANSPARENCIES.** You may want to make transparencies of many of the student materials at the back of this book for instructional use on an overhead projector. Particular pages recommended for this approach are noted with the individual activities.

6. **SMALL INDIVIDUAL CHARTS.** Many activities require students to have their own copies of the pictorial, numeral, or blank charts. Duplicate the two small pictorial charts (pages 89–90) and the numeral and blank charts (pages 91–92) back to back on colored cardstock and laminate them. If you want students to have a pictorial chart with flaps, duplicate the chart on page 89 separately and cut off the strip on the right. Then turn the strip face down, tape it in place, and cut the flaps.

7. **SMALL NUMBER CARDS.** To make sets of small pictorial and numeral cards for the students, duplicate the pictorial chart (page 90) and the numeral chart (page 91) on two colors of cardstock. Underline the numbers 6, 9, 16, 18, 19, 61, 66, 68, 69, 81, 86, 89, 91, 96, 98, and 99 on the numeral chart; then cut the squares apart. Store each set in a plastic bag. You may want each student to have his or her own set, or you can keep all the sets together for classroom use. Since the cards are small, use them only with older primary children.

8. PUZZLES. Duplicate small pictorial and numeral charts on cardstock and cut them into vertical and horizontal strips to make *number line puzzles* (10 strips in each puzzle). Cut other such charts into about 12 pieces of irregular shape to make *jigsaw puzzles*. (Each such puzzle piece should contain 8 or 9 squares.) Glue a magazine picture on the back of each chart before cutting it into pieces to make the puzzle self-correcting. After students have completed the puzzle, they can turn it over (between two books) to see the picture. These puzzles are good activities for a learning center.

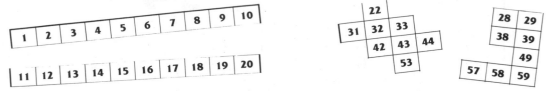

9. FLASH CARDS. Make flash cards by duplicating pages 94–99 on several colors of cardstock and cutting the cards apart. Fifteen sets of each should be plenty for a classroom. Store sets in plastic bags for students to keep at their desks, or store them all together in a central location.

10. EXPANDED NOTATION CARDS. To make expanded notation cards, duplicate page 100 on two colors of cardstock. Cut the cards apart on the solid lines and combine 10 to 90 in one color and 1 to 9 in the other color to make a set. Store sets in plastic bags for students to keep at their desks, or store them all together in a central location.

11. SIGN CIRCLES. To make relational and operational signs (>, <, =, ≠, +, and −) for use with the number cards, duplicate pages 101–102 on cardstock and cut out the circles. Use the large signs with number cards made from the *large* pictorial and numeral charts and use the small signs with number cards made from the *small* charts. Store a few of each of the small signs with the sets of cards made from the small charts. Note that the dot on each > and < sign circle is the eye on a face with an open mouth. This helps the students orient each sign right side up.

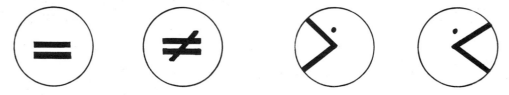

12. MATS. Duplicate the various mats (pages 103–108) on tagboard and laminate them. Students will use the mats in activities teaching place value, addition and subtraction, and money. If you do not laminate the mats, have acetate sheets available when using them (see item 27, below). Students can keep their own mats at their desks, or you can store them all together.

13. SPINNERS. Make two or three of each set of *double spinners* (pages 109–112) for classroom use. Cut out both spinner tops, glue them to a 6″ × 10″ piece of railroad board, and laminate the board. Poke a hole through the center of each spinner. Place a paper clip over each hole and insert a brad fastener through each clip and into the hole. These spinners will store flat and spin easily. If you don't fasten the brads too tightly, you will not need washers. Make two or three of each *single spinner* (pages 113–114) for classroom use. Follow the same procedure described for making the double spinners, using a 6″ × 6″ piece of railroad board for each spinner.

14. MONEY CUT-OUTS. Make money cut-outs by duplicating pages 115–117 on green cardstock and cutting on the dotted lines. Make a complete set for each student and store the sets in individual plastic bags or all together as a class set. Realistic play money and head and tail coin stamps (rubber stamps) can be purchased; both are suggested for several activities.

15. BASE TEN MANIPULATIVES. Students will need base ten manipulatives for the prerequisite activities in Part 3. It is advantageous to provide students with as many kinds of manipulatives as possible; suggestions for making several different kinds follow. You may want to have each student keep a set of base ten manipulatives and about 25 loose beans in a plastic bag; or, keep all the base ten manipulatives together in a class supply. Good commercial base ten materials include powers of ten, base ten blocks, multilinks, and base ten place value stamps. They can be purchased from various suppliers of educational materials.

Ten-beansticks. The advantages of having students make their own beansticks cannot be overemphasized. When students make these items for themselves, they *know* the beansticks are sets of ten. You will need newspaper to work on, Popsicle sticks, pinto beans, and all-purpose white glue (*not* paste or rubber cement). Help students make ten-beansticks by putting a strip of glue down the center of each stick. Students then count out and place ten beans along the glue. Later in the day, add another strip of glue *over* the beans so they will be secure. To make the one hundred flat, glue ten sticks perpendicular to two other sticks, forming a raft. Then have students glue ten beans to each of the ten sticks, just as they did for the individual ten-beansticks. Have each student make at least ten beansticks and one flat. To use sticks on an overhead projector, drill holes in place of the beans.

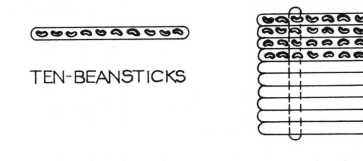

TEN-BEANSTICKS

Ten-cartons. Ask each student to bring an empty egg carton from home. Cut off two of the egg compartments to make a 2 × 5 compartment carton. These cartons can be used to make sets of ten by placing *one* bean in each hole or to make a set of one hundred by placing *ten* beans in each hole.

Ten-frames. To make ten-frames, you will need ½" wire mesh (rabbit pen), wire cutters, tagboard, and all-purpose white glue. Cut the wire mesh into strips containing ten squares in a 2 × 5 configuration. Cut tagboard into rectangles about 2" × 3½" each. Place the wire frame on the tagboard and squeeze a generous portion of glue around the four edges of the frame to attach it. Be sure to cover any rough or sharp edges with glue to keep the frames safe. Also cut a few 10 × 10 mesh squares to make a one hundred flat. Pinto beans or multibase ones will fit into the squares.

These ten-frames are wonderful for regrouping activities in addition and subtraction. They are also good for teaching odd and even. To use the frames on an overhead projector, use a wire frame that has not been glued to tagboard.

Ten-felt-boards. Glue ten circles of the same color of felt in a 5 × 2 arrangement on a 3" × 6" rectangle of felt in another color. Make ten of these felt boards. Then cut nine loose circles of the same color felt as the circles glued on the boards.

½" WIRE MESH WIRE GLUED ON TAGBOARD

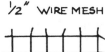
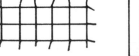

TEN-FRAMES

TEN-FELT BOARDS

Ten-canisters. Children can easily make ten-canisters with empty film canisters (for 35 mm film) and lima beans. Have them count out ten lima beans for each canister, then close the lid to create a set of ten. When using these canisters in activities that involve renaming, have some empty canisters and loose beans available. Use a larger canister with a lid to make a set of one hundred.

Ten-cups. Use small paper cups in place of the film canisters for making sets of ten. Then you can use a larger styrofoam cup for the set of one hundred. Check fast food chains for several sizes of cups with lids.

16. GIANT CHARTS. Use a black marking pen or laundry pen to make a giant 10 × 10 grid on each of two standard-size flat bedding sheets. Make the individual squares about 8″ × 9″. On one sheet, write each of the numerals 1 to 100, making a giant numeral 1 to 100 chart; leave the other sheet as a blank grid. Then make several 2 × 10 grids with 9½″ × 9½″ squares, using masking tape on an 8′ × 19″ black plastic ground cover. Leave the squares empty for graphing or building portions of the 1 to 100 charts with place value manipulatives.

17. ACTIVE GAME NUMBER CARDS. For active classroom games, make five sets of 1 to 100 cards on 8½″ × 5½″ pieces of construction paper. Use five colors of paper for the five different categories shown below:

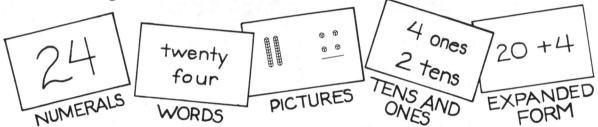

18. TRIANGULAR EXPANDED NOTATION CARDS. Make these by cutting six equilateral triangles from a 9″ × 12″ piece of tagboard. For each card, write numbers in the corners using black and red pens as shown below. Make about 30 of these cards for various numbers between 11 and 99. Include all the teen numbers and all the numbers in which the digits of the teen numbers are reversed (for example, 13 and 31). Laminate the cards.

19. MONEY CARDS. To make money cards as shown below, divide 4″ × 7″ cards into three sections across. Using coin rubber stamps, stamp some dimes and pennies in heads and tails in the far left section. Write the words *dimes* and *pennies* at the top of the other two sections. Make the cards self-correcting by writing the coin amount on the back of the card. Write the answers in both cent and dollar notation; for example, 37¢ and $0.37. Laminate each card.

	dimes	pennies

20. GEOBOARDS. Make several 10 × 10 geoboards using 11" × 11" pieces of plywood and 100 nails for each board. Use inch graph paper to get the nails in the correct places. Label one hundred plastic bread-bag fasteners with the numerals 1 to 100. You may want to use two or three colors of fasteners and label the numerals in a pattern. (For example, for an even-odd pattern, you could label all yellow fasteners with odd numbers and all blue fasteners with even numbers.)

21. PAPER PLATE PUZZLES. Make these puzzles by stamping or drawing a picture of tens and ones in a recognized pattern on the left half of a paper plate and writing the corresponding numeral on the right half of the plate. Cut each plate into a two-part puzzle. Make each set of ten puzzles a different color, as follows:

Set A (color A): 10, 20, 30, ..., 100 (decade numbers)
Set B (color B): 21–30 or 46–55 (ten consecutive numbers)
Set C (color C): ten random numbers from 1 to 100

22. DOT PATTERN PLATES. Prepare a set of paper plates with dot patterns for the numbers 0 to 10. Use dinner-sized plates to make a teacher set and luncheon-sized plates to make several student sets. Draw large dot patterns on the plates with a felt-tip marker and a circle template. Make several different patterns for each number so students will learn to associate more than one pattern with any given number. However, dots should always appear in rows of *four or fewer* so students can identify the sets by sight, without counting.

EXAMPLES:

23. PATTERN BEANSTICKS. Glue two kinds of beans (dark and light) to wooden sticks in all combinations of the numbers from 0 to 10 without putting more than four or five beans of one kind in a row. (The eye can see only groups of *five or fewer* without counting.) Have students use these beansticks to practice recognizing combinations in patterns without counting.

24. FACT FAMILY CARDS. Duplicate centimeter graph paper on cardstock. For each number to 20, make a pictorial drill card with all the combinations for that number. Illustrate each combination with a solid and striped set of squares that together equal the number for that card. These cards are handy for a quick verbal drill or for having students write all the fact family combinations.

EXAMPLE:

$$2 + 4 = 6$$
$$4 + 2 = 6$$
$$6 - 2 = 4$$
$$6 - 4 = 2$$

Fact family for the first grid (top left)

25. PICK-UP STICKS. Make these by drawing ten dots—five in one color, five in another color—on one side of a Popsicle stick and one dot on the other side of the stick. Make 30 to 40 of these place value pick-up sticks. When students toss a handful of these sticks, some will show their ten side and some will show their one side. Students can then sort and count them to find the total amount for that toss.

26. MARKERS OR CHIPS. Obtain about 50 clear, colored plastic game markers (chips) for each student. Students might store their own sets (each set in a single color) in a film canister, or you may store them all together for class use.

27. ACETATE SHEETS. In the activities we often suggest that a worksheet or chart be placed under an acetate sheet, especially in a game where crayons are used to indicate a play or an answer. This saves on paper, allowing the worksheet or chart to be used again and again. Use only the heaviest acetate sheets available. The heaviest weatherization film purchased at a hardware store is the most durable type; it does not crack, but stays soft and pliable. Cut each sheet to the size of your backing tagboard. Use masking tape to attach the acetate to the tagboard along one edge. Use an old sock or a small carpet piece (nap down) to wipe crayon off the acetate sheet (or from any laminated materials).

Prerequisite Activities

Students' understanding of numbers should grow out of experiences with patterns and sorting, ordering, grouping, and comparing objects. As students explore such relationships, they learn number patterns and their need to count diminishes. They internalize number concepts, and the foundation for understanding our number system has been laid. Do not hurry through these prerequisite activities with younger primary children. You will see the payoff later when you begin to use the charts for numeration and place value, addition and subtraction, multiplication and division, and money. It is better to nurture a broad base of experience than to be guilty of forced blooming.

1. Looking for Patterns

Objective: Pattern awareness

Grade level: 1–3

Group size: Whole class

Procedure: At the beginning of the year, encourage students to find patterns, designs, groupings, or arrangements in nature and objects familiar to them.

Have students bring in leaves, flowers, pine cones, feathers, and shells to observe patterns in nature. Discuss how leaves from one kind of tree have the same pattern and how flowers of one kind have the same design, regardless of color or size. Have students bring in examples of patterns in fabric, quilts, pieces of wallpaper, or pictures of tile from home. Talk about the designs and what it would look like to continue each pattern. Students can also look around the classroom and school building for patterns in brickwork, windows, lights, floor tile, and fence posts.

Display nature pictures, fabric samples, and number or shape patterns in the room. Have students tell you about one of the patterns, show you a pattern they like, or turn away and tell you about one of the patterns from memory. Encourage students to observe and discuss patterns they see in clothing, fingerprints, their daily routine, musical rhythms, or the cycle of the seasons.

2. Experiencing Patterns (Active)

Objective: Involvement in patterns

Grade level: 1–3

Group size: Whole class

Materials: Pattern blocks, multilinks, macaroni, shells, buttons, crayons, coins, small chips, tile, or other materials for building patterns; geoboards (see page 11) and multilinks or cut-out squares; giant 2 × 10 grids (see page 10); materials for art projects

Procedure: Try to have students experience a pattern sometime during each day so that patterns become part of their awareness and thinking.

Auditory patterns. Slowly repeat a snap-clap-tap-stomp pattern. (When you first do this activity, use only two or three actions.) Have students join you *only* when they hear the pattern for themselves. Repeat the pattern until all feel and hear the rhythm. Part of the time verbalize with the actions, saying, for example "snap, clap, clap, snap, clap, clap..." or "one, three, three, one, three, three..." or "c, g, g, c, g, g..." or "Sue, Jim, Jim, Sue, Jim, Jim...." Labeling a pattern helps organize it. For auditory memory, ask students to close their eyes, concentrate on hearing the pattern, wait a bit, and then repeat the pattern themselves.

Physical patterns. Use students to create a sit-sit-stand-sit-sit-stand pattern. Or lead an action-filled pattern with twisting, touching parts of the body, and using different rhythmic methods: hop, step, hop, hop, step, hop...; touch your head, ear, knee, head, ear, knee, head.... Students like to be the leader and start a pattern for other students to follow. Keep the patterns simple at first and then gradually increase the complexity. Ask students to perform a series of three or four sequenced steps. Say, for example, "Touch your nose, walk to the sink, clap three times, return to your seat, (repeat)...." If students have difficulty, include fewer steps or ask them to repeat the steps orally. Draw a pattern on the chalkboard and have students continue the pattern on paper at their desks. Some possible patterns are shown below.

⊤ ⊣ ⊥ ⊥ ⊤ ⊣ · · ·

5 3 1 5 3 1 5 3 · · ·

A K L P A K L P A · · ·

○ △ □ ○ △ □ · · ·

d d b l p d d b l p d d · · ·

Object and shape patterns.   Have students use pattern blocks, multilinks, macaroni, shells, buttons, crayons, coins, or other materials to build a simple pattern, repeat it, and keep repeating it. Children like to start a pattern and have a friend continue it. It's important to verbalize and put action to the patterns. For example, when students build a pattern with multilinks, they can say the colors aloud ("red, blue, blue, yellow, red, blue, blue, yellow, red...") and then give it a rhythmic pattern (snap, clap, clap, tap, snap, clap, clap, tap, snap...). Combine the visual, auditory, and kinesthetic all at once when possible. For visual memory, show a pattern, remove it, wait a bit, and then have students build and continue that pattern. Begin with linear patterns that can be extended in one line or extended on grids from row to row. Later, have students create two-dimensional designs with lines of symmetry and reflections. Use a geoboard with multilinks over the nails or with cut-out squares laid on it. You can suggest to students to start with a common border *or* have all the corners the same *or* move out from the center.

Patterns that grow.   Create a pattern on the chalkboard or an overhead projector and ask students to build and continue it using small chips, tiles, or multilinks. Make the patterns as easy or hard as you want. See if students can identify a number pattern to match the chip pattern. Some examples are shown below.

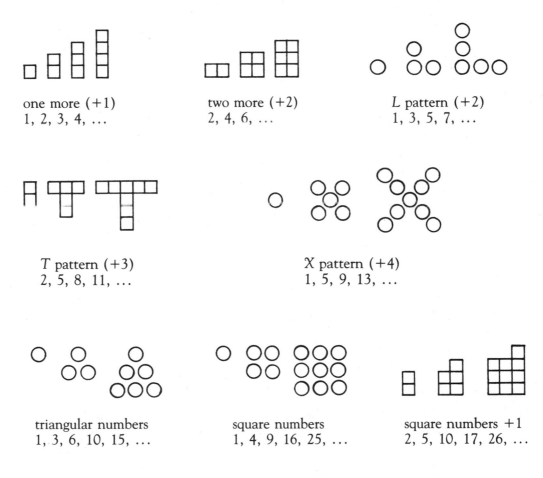

one more (+1)
1, 2, 3, 4, ...

two more (+2)
2, 4, 6, ...

L pattern (+2)
1, 3, 5, 7, ...

T pattern (+3)
2, 5, 8, 11, ...

X pattern (+4)
1, 5, 9, 13, ...

triangular numbers
1, 3, 6, 10, 15, ...

square numbers
1, 4, 9, 16, 25, ...

square numbers +1
2, 5, 10, 17, 26, ...

Graphing.   Graphing organizes data in a pattern that can then be interpreted. Graph such things as color of eyes or hair; kind of shoes; who's having cold lunch, hot lunch, or going home; favorite crackers, ice creams, seasons, TV shows. Use several of the giant 2 × 10 grids, laid side by side, to make graphs with primary students. They can stand on the grid as they gather data.

Guess my rule. Use a "guess my rule" activity to have students search for patterns. This is a quick activity good for beginning the day or filling extra minutes. Ask students to give you a number less than 10 and give them a number back according to your rule. Then students should try to guess the rule. Older students can graph the information to help them draw conclusions and then write a formula. (Possible rules: add 1, add 2, subtract 1, double the number, triple the number and add 1, subtract the number from 8.)

RULE: +1   □ + 1 = △

listed at random

□	△
6	7
2	3
9	10
5	6
1	2
3	4
4	–
8	–
7	–

reorganize the data to see the pattern more clearly

□	△
1	2
2	3
3	4
4	5
5	6
6	7
7	–

Pattern art projects. Ideas for art projects with linear patterns include macaroni necklaces, paper chains, or woven mats. Students can use graph paper and colors to create a design within a given area. Border patterns for stationery or placemats are also fun. When students are making border patterns, have them first lay out their pattern with objects before actually pasting it down or drawing it. You may also want to provide mirrors so students can see lines of symmetry and reflections. Help students to see order and patterns within their own creations. After all the projects are finished, talk about them with the class. Ask, for example, "What do you see in Sue's design? Is there a pattern to Tom's chain?"

3. 0 to 9 Number Patterns and More

Objective: Knowledge of familiar number patterns *without* counting

Grade level: 1–3

Group size: Whole class; small groups or individuals at a learning center

Materials: 3 × 3 and 5 × 2 grids (page 93), game markers, flash cards (pages 94–97), regular decks of cards, dot pattern plates (see page 11), sign circles (pages 101–102), pattern beansticks (see page 11), and fact family graph cards (see page 11)

Procedure: Although students' earliest experiences with number operations are based on counting, they must internalize number knowledge and eventually divorce themselves from the need to count in every number situation. For example, if students add three objects to four objects by counting from 1 to 7, they are counting, not adding. Knowing and using arrangement patterns without counting each dot will help students in computation. It is important for students to learn to recognize numbers in different arrangements.

Regular domino pattern. Teach the regular domino pattern for 0 to 9 using the game markers on the 3 × 3 grid. Have students build each number from 0 to 9 in the sequence shown below and repeat that until they understand the pattern. To check knowledge of the domino pattern call out numbers at random and have students build the number on their grids.

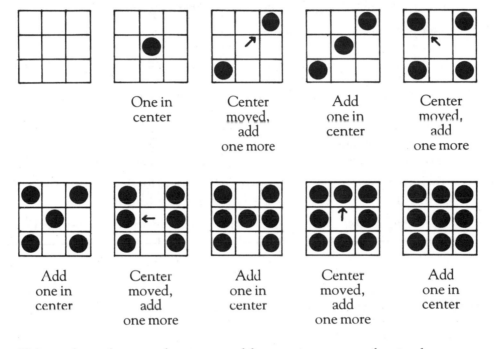

| One in center | Center moved, add one more | Add one in center | Center moved, add one more |

| Add one in center | Center moved, add one more | Add one in center | Center moved, add one more | Add one in center |

Help students discover the pattern of first putting one marker in the center and then moving the chip out of the center and adding one more. Use the regular domino flash cards for drill.

Modified domino pattern. Teach the modified domino pattern for 1 to 10 using the game markers on the double 3 × 3 grid (6 × 3). Have students build 1 to 5 in the upper 3 × 3 grid and then build 6 to 10 as "5 plus some more."

This pattern uses the "5 plus some more" concept. Also, you'll notice the ones increase by one more each time but never change their position in space. This pattern is used on the pictorial charts. Use the modified domino flash cards for drill.

Ten-frame pattern. Teach the ten-frame pattern for 0 to 20 using the game markers with the 5 × 2 grid for 0 to 10 and the double 5 × 2 grid (5 × 4) for 11 to 20. (Or use ten-frames made from wire mesh, as described on page 9.) Have students build the numbers 0 to 20. See the ten-frame flash cards on page 97 for a possible arrangement of the chips. Students can have different arrangements as long as they can recognize the number at a glance. This pattern builds on the "5 plus some more" concept. After you have two 5's, you have "10 plus some more" for 11 to 20. (See part 1, page 4 for help in teaching the numbers 11 to 19.) Use the ten-frame flash cards for drill.

To reinforce knowledge of the regular and modified domino patterns and the ten-frame pattern, use them on bingo cards. Or, use two sets of the flash cards to play concentration.

Playing card patterns. Use regular decks of playing cards and have students observe the pattern arrangements on the numbered cards. Have them drill each other for quick recognition of these number patterns.

Dot pattern plates. Use the dot pattern plates at the learning center for activities involving one-to-one correspondence (matching chips or clothespins to the dots), sorting, sequencing, and making number sentences with the sign symbols. Teach the commutative property by switching the plates in the sentences. The large plates are also good for classroom drill. Ask such questions as, "What do you see? What number is what you see plus one more? plus two more? What number is what you see minus one? minus two? What number is what you see doubled?" Cover some of the dots and drill for the missing addend. Say, for example, "This is a seven plate. What part is missing?"

Beanstick patterns. Use the pattern beansticks for the same kinds of activities as the dot pattern plates with small groups at a learning center.

Picturing combinations. Use fact family graph cards for drilling fact families. These work best for verbal drill in small groups or for having individual students write the fact family combinations at a learning center.

4. Grouping Galore

Objective: Experience in grouping

Grade level: 1–2

Group size: Whole class, working in pairs

Materials: Lima beans, bottle caps, cotton balls, washers, bread tags, nuts, or other materials for counting; jars of different sizes; small cups; multilinks; and place value manipulatives (see pages 9–10)

Procedure: Experiencing grouping activities lays the foundation for students' understanding of place value and multiplication. This activity gives students practice in counting by twos, fives, or tens.

Have students take a handful of lima beans, bottle caps, counters, or other materials, estimate how many they have, and then place them into small cups in groups of tens, fives, or twos to find out. Tell them to record the counts in pictorial or numeral form and then group the objects in another way to see if they get the same amount. Or, have them give the objects to a friend to check the count.

Have students estimate the amount of objects (cotton balls, washers, bread tags, nuts) in jars of different sizes. Then have them group the objects from each jar into small cups to count them. After recording their amounts, they can have them checked by switching jars with a friend who should group the objects in another way to count them.

Have students build a long stick using one color of multilinks and then estimate how many there are in the stick. The stick may then be broken into groups to get the actual count. Again, students can record their counts and then have a friend check by grouping in another way.

Let students each make some ten-beansticks and some ten-canisters. You can cut the ten-cartons and make the ten-frames. You will want these manipulatives available for place value activities. Follow up the manipulative activities with random pictures of things to be grouped by tens, fives, or twos. Students should write down how many there are and then switch with a friend for checking. Laminated pictures can be used repeatedly. At Christmas, have students estimate and then make tree chains of red and green fives or tens.

5. Sequence to 100

Objective: Understanding of the "one more" pattern and tens and ones

Grade level: 1–2

Group size: Whole class

Materials: A bell, a marking pen, and some 1-foot wide butcher paper (long enough to record pictorially to 100) divided down the center with a line, multilinks in one color or loose beans with ten small paper cups, ten-cartons, or ten-canisters (see pages 9–10); acetate sheets, crayons and wipes, place value mats (page 103), 3" × 5" cards, and small blank charts (page 92)

Procedure: Draw two rows of five X's on the 3" × 5" cards and place them on the right side of the place value mats. Then place the mats and the cards under the acetate sheets. Record the numbers 1 to 100 pictorially on the butcher paper as the students build them on their place value mats. Each time you ring the bell, students should add one more multilink to the right side of their mat. Whenever students have ten loose multilinks placed on the X's on the right side of the mat, they must gather them, stick them together as a set of ten, and place them on the left side of the mat. (If students are using loose beans and small cups, they should gather the ten loose beans to make a cup of ten.) Students will see how the numbers increase by one each time, and how to group and rename ten loose ones into a set of ten. Draw the pictures of ones on the right side of the butcher paper and the pictures of tens on the left side in patterns easily recognized by the children, dots and sticks. Ask students to say each number's meaning aloud before the next ring (1 ten 2 ones, for example). When you draw 10 ones for the decade numbers, cross out the picture and then draw 1 ten in the left column. Continue this activity over a period of several weeks until you reach 100. Circle and look for patterns on the large strip. Use different manipulatives for variety.

After you have completed the activity as a class, have students make their own 1 to 100 picture strips and complete them over a period of a month. Cut strips two squares wide from the small blank chart and tape them together to make the strips. Students should build each number, record it in numerals with a crayon, and then draw the picture as they say the number to themselves. Have them draw ones as dots or X's, tens as a stick or cup.

Variation

For more advanced students, try this same activity in base 5 using different names: 3 ones, 4 ones, 5 ones or 1 quint, 1 quint 1 one, 1 quint 2 ones .... (The 3" × 5" card would have only five X's.) When you reach 4 quints 4 ones, you can go backwards to 0 again by giving one away with each bell ring and breaking up the sets of five. Compare the large pictorial strip for base 5 with the strip for base 10, looking for patterns and similarities.

6. Fair Trade to 100

Objective: Experience in grouping by tens

Grade level: 1–2 (Variation 4: 3–4)

Group size: Whole class, divided into small groups

Materials: Dice; place value manipulatives in hundreds, tens, and ones—loose beans and ten-beansticks, ten-canisters, ten-cups, ten-frames, ten-cartons, or commercial base ten blocks, and a few one hundred sets of each manipulative (see pages 9–10); place value mats (page 103) with 3″ × 5″ cards with 10 X's and acetate sheets as described in Activity 5; crayons and wipes; and for Variation 3, expanded notation cards (page 100) and one of the double spinners (pages 109–112)

Procedure: Go over the rules of the game. You may want to show how it is played using an overhead projector and a transparency of the place value mat. Explain that whenever a player has ten loose beans placed on the X's, the player must gather them and make a trade for a set of ten. The loose beans (ones) are placed on the right side of the mat; the tens are placed on the left side of the mat. Then divide the class into small groups. Players take turns rolling the dice and collecting the number of beans to match their roll. Then they place the beans on their mat, making a trade if necessary. After all the players have had a turn, each should state how many beans are showing on his or her mat. ("I have 3 ten-sticks and 4 loose beans; ten, twenty, thirty, thirty-one, thirty-two, thirty-three, thirty-four." Or, "I have thirty plus four, which is 34.") Ask, "How many cups or tens do you have? How many loose beans or ones? If you dumped all of your beans into one pile, how many would you have?" Play continues with players taking turns, collecting loose beans, and making fair trades until someone trades 10 sets of ten for a set of 100 to win the game. Play this game often until students are comfortable making trades of 10 loose ones for a set of ten.

Variation 1

Everyone begins with a set of 100 beans and they give away what they roll each time. Before they can give away any beans, players will need to break the set of 100 into 10 sets of ten and then trade a set of ten for 10 loose beans. Be sure students understand that they still have 100 beans on their mat, they have just renamed them so that some can be given away. At the end of each player's turn, the player should state the amount still showing on the mat.

Variation 2

Try this variation without the 3″ × 5″ card on the right side of the mat. In addition to building what is rolled each time, players should draw pictures with crayon on the acetate. (Sticks for sets of ten, dots for loose ones.) They will need to wipe the acetate to remove pictures of loose beans when they trade 10 loose beans for a set of ten. Some students find it helpful to draw a picture of their roll as all ones. Then they can circle a set of 10 loose beans, erase the set, and add a ten-stick picture. All players should say aloud what they have at the end of each turn.

Variation 3

Use the expanded notation cards along with pictures and recorded numerals. If a player has drawn a picture of 34, he or she should record 34 on the acetate at the bottom of the mat and lay the card for 30 below the tens side and the card for 4 below the ones side, saying, "I have 30 plus 4, which is 34." Then the player can push the two expanded cards together so that each digit is in its place. In this example, the 3 is really 3 tens, or 30. The 0 in 30 is there, you just don't see it when the 4 card is over it. After each roll, players add to their drawings, record the numeral at the bottom of the mat, and use the expanded notation cards to represent the new number.

Variation 4

Third and fourth graders can play this game until they have a set of 1,000. Use one of the double spinners so the game can progress quickly. Make some 100, 200 ... 900 cards in a third color to add to the set of expanded notation cards. Make a place value mat with three sections for hundreds, tens, and ones. (You could also use three colors of game markers to represent hundreds, tens, and ones, but this is abstract and should be done only if students already understand place value.)

7.   Odd and Even

Objective: Understanding of odd and even and counting by twos

Grade level: 1–3

Group size: Whole class

Materials: Ten-frames (see page 9) and loose beans (or ten-cartons and multilinks); multilinks

Procedure: Each student should have four ten-frames. Tell the students to build consecutive numbers from 1 to 40 using beans in ten-frames. After students reach the number 10, they can add another ten-frame. Have them keep building numbers consecutively, adding ten-frames as needed. Talk about the meaning of odd (not having a partner, the "oddball") and the meaning of even (having a partner). When students build numbers in a ten-frame, they can see the pattern of odd, even, odd, even, odd ... develop. Allow enough time and enough building for students to really understand the concept of odd and even. (For young children the ten-cartons and multilinks would be easier to use. Or, use the children's bodies.)

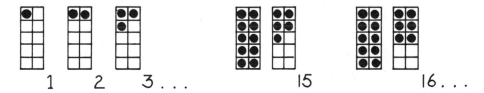

$$1 \quad\quad 2 \quad\quad 3 \ldots \quad\quad\quad 15 \quad\quad\quad 16 \ldots$$

Another way to teach about odd and even numbers is to form a line of multilinks by adding one each day. Build them in pairs in a long row. Use a different color of multilinks for each new group of ten days. Students can see at a glance if the number for that day is odd or even, and they can count the number quickly as some tens plus some more. Have students practice counting by twos each day as you point to the paired multilinks. When you reach 100, join the multilinks into a 10 × 10 flat.

Matching fingertips is another way to make odd and even obvious. Tell students to close both hands to begin with. For one, a thumb is raised; it has no partner so it is odd. For two, both thumbs are put together; they are partners so two is even. For three, put up an index finger; it has no partner so it is odd. For four, add the other index finger; the index fingers are partners, so four is even. Students can keep putting up one more finger with each number. They will see that when the fingertips are matched, the numbers are even. When another is added and has no partner, that number is odd. When determining whether a number such as 23 is odd or even, have students tap together all their fingertips and say "ten," do it again and say, "20," and then go on—"twenty-one, twenty-two, twenty-three"—raising one finger each time. Give a number, ask if it is odd or even, then ask students to prove it. The fingertip method is easy to use. Ask, "How can you tell if a number is odd or even?" Hopefully students will understand why we look at the ones digit to determine whether a number is odd or even.

Numeration and Place Value Activities

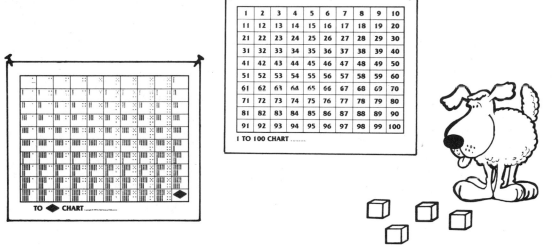

The charts and place value activities in Part 4 will give students added understanding of numbers 1 to 100. Often children begin to have an intuitive feel for our number system, but we don't give them enough time to construct internal equilibrium through their own actions on objects. It is known from Piaget's research that the cognitive structures of the mind are self-regulating when they are given enough time and experience. Many teachers provide good manipulative materials in teaching concepts but do not spend enough time with visual pictures that represent those concrete objects. The pictorial chart can help you spend enough time with the visual pictures so that your students can gain lasting understanding.

We suggest that you reread the section in Part 1 (page 4) concerning the numbers from 11 to 19. Special attention needs to be given to these numbers.

8. What Do You See?

Objective: Awareness of the wholeness of and the patterns in the numeration system

Grade level: 1–3

Group size: Small group

Materials: Large pictorial and numeral charts posted where students can see them, small pictorial and numeral charts (pages 89–91)

Procedure: Introduce the large pictorial chart by asking students, "What do you see?" You may want to bring small groups of students to the chart on the wall or distribute a small pictorial chart to each student. Encourage students to observe the following:

- The sticks and cubes represent tens and ones.
- The number of cubes in a square grows by one in each square as you move across a row to the right.
- The number of ten sticks in a square stays the same in each square of a given row.
- The number of ones in a square stays the same in each square of a given column.
- The number of ten sticks in a square grows by one in each square as you move down a column.
- Tens and ones are grouped by "five plus some more."
- The flaps show a second name for each decade number.
- One hundred has three names.
- The ones do not change position as the numbers increase.

Introduce the large numeral chart by asking again, "What do you see?" Encourage students to describe patterns and relationships they see on the chart, just as they did on the pictorial chart. Then have students answer the following two questions, using the numeral chart if necessary:

- How many times would you use the digit 9 to number the pages of a 99-page book? (20)
- Suppose you tore pages 8, 9, 63, and 64 out of a book. How many separate sheets of paper would you have? (3)

Variation
At the third grade level, the whole class could be involved at once. Use transparencies of the charts on an overhead projector and distribute copies of the small pictorial and numeral charts. Refer to Activities 64, 79, 80, and 81 for further ideas for discovering patterns and relationships on these charts.

9. Building the Chart Sequence to 100

Objective: Familiarity with the tens and ones configurations on the chart

Grade level: 1–2

Group size: Whole class, divided into small groups

Materials: A bell, base ten blocks in tens and ones with a few hundreds available, or loose beans and ten-beansticks with a few one hundred flats available (see page 9), tens and ones mats (page 104), flash cards (pages 94–99); and for the variation, the large blank chart (see page 7)

Procedure: After discussing the pictorial chart, have students build the configurations on the chart in order to learn what number each picture represents without counting. Each time you ring the bell, have students add a one to the mat according to the modified domino pattern (see Activity 3). When they have 10 loose ones on the right side of the mat, the students can gather them and trade them for a ten-stick to place at the top left side of the mat. Have students continue adding ones and trading until they have built 100. Then have them give away tens and ones back to 0. Stop frequently to ask, "What is showing on your mat now?" (For example, 4 tens, 2 ones; 42.) Use the pictorial flash cards to drill chart patterns. Or, use all the flash cards on pages 94–97 to review or sort the number patterns.

Variation

You may want to build the configurations on an overhead projector as students build them at their desks. Or, you may want to use the large blank chart in front of the room to write each numeral on the chart after you ring the bell and students have built the number. Or, try using children with a tape grid on the floor. When ten is reached, students can join hands for a set of "ten."

10. Building a 1 to 100 Chart (Active)

Objective:	Working with tens and ones
Grade level:	1–2
Group size:	Small group
Materials:	Giant 10 × 10 blank chart (see page 10) and a large amount of base ten manipulatives (see pages 9–10)
Procedure:	Have small groups of students work together to build a giant 1 to 100 chart using base ten materials in the hall, gym, or corner of the room. Have them place 1 one in the first square, 2 ones in the second square, and so on until they reach 100. Encourage students to place the materials down in patterns so that they can recognize any number at a glance. This activity provides students with good practice in sequencing numbers and trading ones for a set of ten when they reach each decade.

11. Building Part of a 1 to 100 Chart (Active)

Objective:	Working with tens and ones
Grade level:	1–2
Group size:	Individuals
Materials:	Giant 2 × 10 blank chart (see page 10), large pictorial and numeral number line strips (see page 6), and base ten manipulatives (see pages 9–10)
Procedure:	Have students on the floor. Ask each student to choose two consecutive strips (1–20, 11–30, 21–40, 31–50, and so on) and to build those numbers with manipulatives. Children need to experience the growing by "one more" of our numeration system and to practice fair trading when they encounter ten ones. Students should place the materials on the chart so that they can recognize a number at a glance. If you have a walking number line, you could also use that for building a sequence of consecutive numbers.

12. Building and Recording Numbers at Random

Objective:	Working with tens and ones
Grade level:	1–3
Group size:	Whole class
Materials:	Base ten manipulatives (see pages 9–10), place value mats (page 103), and one of the double spinners (pages 109–112) or a set of "active game" cards (see page 10), expanded notation cards (page 8), acetate sheets, and crayons and wipes
Procedure:	Spin the spinner (or draw a card) and call out the number. Tell students to

build that number on their mats and to record its numeral form. "Clear your mat!" Spin again, and build the number with manipulatives so that students can see your work. Students should observe your number and then build and record it themselves. Interchange the auditory and visual procedure. Build and record numbers as long as necessary for students to get a good grasp of tens and ones. Then set the manipulatives aside and just draw pictures and record the numerals. Next, add the expanded notation cards so that each number you spin is drawn pictorially, recorded numerically, and represented with the expanded notation cards. (See Activity 6, Variation 3 for details on how to use the expanded notation cards.) This activity could also be done in small groups with a leader who spins, calls out the number, and checks answers for accuracy.

Variation
For third graders, use hundreds, tens, and ones. Use a mat with three sections for hundreds, tens, and ones.

13. Flannelboard Match

Objective: Matching and counting tens and ones

Grade level: 1–2

Group size: Individuals

Materials: Ten-felt-boards and loose circles (see page 9), pictorial and numeral cards made from the large charts (see page 6)

Procedure: Demonstrate this activity for the whole class, then use it for a learning center activity. Select a pictorial (or numeral) card. Represent the amount on the flannelboard using the felt tens and the loose felt circles. Encourage students to place the loose ones in an easily recognized pattern. Then count the amount—"ten, twenty, thirty, thirty-one, thirty-two, thirty-three"—and express it verbally in expanded form—"thirty plus three is thirty-three."

14. Tens and Ones Pick-up Sticks (Active)

Objective: Counting tens and ones; understanding of more or less

Grade level: 1–2

Group size: Two players

Materials: Tens and ones pick-up sticks (see page 12), small pictorial charts (page 90), and a die with *more* and *less* written on the sides

Procedure: Have students play this game in pairs. Each player drops ten pick-up sticks, sorts them, and counts the amount shown. Then one player throws the more or less die. If *less* shows, the player with the smaller amount gets a point for that round; if *more* shows, the player with the greater amount gets the point. The player gets an extra point if he or she can find that amount on the small pictorial chart. Play continues for a predetermined number of rounds or points.

Variation 1
Individual students can play this game alone; dropping the sticks, recording the amount, and finding it on the chart.

Variation 2
If three students play the game, the player with neither the highest nor the lowest amount gets the point for each round.

Variation 3

Use 15 or more pick-up sticks. Note that regrouping may be necessary, and the total amount may be greater than 100.

15. Make the Number

Objective:	Practice with tens and ones
Grade level:	1–2
Group size:	Individuals
Materials:	Set of numeral cards made from the large chart (see page 6), graph paper, scissors, glue, and scratch paper
Procedure:	Instruct students to select a numeral card, write that numeral on the scratch paper, cut the correct number of ten sticks and ones from the graph paper, and paste them down. Students should make one number on each piece of paper. Encourage students to paste the tens and ones in patterns so the number can be checked at a glance. Each student should make enough numbers to gain the amount of practice he or she needs. You can use the finished papers to drill the whole class. Ask, "What do you see? What number did Sue make?"

16. Putting Together

Objective:	Practice writing expanded notation
Grade level:	1–2
Group size:	Individuals
Materials:	One of the double spinners (pages 109–112), expanded notation cards (page 100), paper, and pencil
Procedure:	This activity provides individual students practice in writing expanded notation sentences. The student spins the tens side of the spinner and records the number. Then the student spins the ones side of the spinner and adds that amount to complete the sentence. Then the student should find the cards for the two numbers and push them together so that they show one number. The whole class could practice this part of the activity using their expanded notation cards. Each student would draw a tens card and a ones card, write the expanded notation sentence, and push the cards together to show one number.

17. Stamping a 1 to 100 Chart (Active)

Objective:	Drawing tens and ones to 100
Grade level:	2–3
Group size:	Whole class
Materials:	Base ten stamps (see page 9), stamp pad, and three or four large pieces of butcher paper ruled with 10 × 10 grids (each square in the grids should be about 4″ × 5″, depending on the size of the stamps); a large pictorial chart or number line strips (see page 6) available for reference, and legal-size paper 8½″ × 14″)
Procedure:	Before starting to work on the large butcher chart, have students practice drawing two rows of the pictorial chart using sticks and dots. Cut sheets of legal-size paper in half and divide each piece into two rows of eleven rectangles.

Give one of these sheets to each student to use for the practice drawing. There are eleven boxes in each row because some students will need to cut a flap in order to show the renaming of the decade numbers; others will show them already renamed and just fold the last box under. Encourage students to draw each number in some kind of pattern so they can recognize it at a glance. This pre-activity will produce better results when each student is given a turn to stamp one row on the 10 × 10 chart. Set up the stamping activity near the large pictorial chart. Have scratch paper available for warm-up or practice. Display the students' charts where they can see them. Discuss which pictures show numbers so they are easily recognized at a glance. Repeat this activity at a later time and compare the results. Activity 24 is a good follow-up to this activity.

18. Stamping Numbers

Objective: Drawing the number before and the number after

Grade level: 1–3

Group size: Small group or individuals

Materials: Base ten stamps (see page 9), stamp pad, paper, numeral or pictorial cards made from the large charts (see page 6), the small pictorial and numeral charts (pages 90–91) available for reference

Procedure: Have each student fold a piece of paper into three parts horizontally or divide it into three parts with a pencil. Then have each student draw a numeral card, stamp a picture of that number in the middle section on their paper, and then stamp the number that comes before and the number that comes after in the other two sections. You could also have students stamp the number they draw in the first or the last section and then stamp the two numbers after or before it in the other two sections. If you need to simplify the activity for your students, have them divide their paper into only two sections and stamp just the number and the number before *or* after it.

Variation 1
Instruct students to divide the paper vertically and stamp the picture of the number they draw in the middle box. Then they can stamp the appropriate numbers in the boxes above and below.

Variation 2
Have students draw a cross with five squares (as shown below) and stamp the number they draw in the middle square. Then they can stamp the numbers that surround it on the pictorial chart in the surrounding squares. If base ten stamps are not available, have the children draw pictures of tens and ones, or simply write numerals.

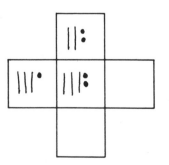

19. Calendar Fun

Objective: Review of number patterns

Grade level: 1–2

Group size: Whole class

Materials: Blank monthly calendar, beans and ten-beansticks (see page 9) or place value stamps (see page 9), and flash cards (pages 94–99) or pictorial cards for the numbers to 31 made from the large chart (see page 6)

Procedure: You can review any of the number patterns or reinforce place value on the calendar. Attach beans and ten-beansticks to a large butcher paper calendar. Or, let one student each day use place value stamps to create the number pattern for that day. You could keep a mixture of flash cards and cards made from the large pictorial chart in a box from which the students could make a selection each day.

Variation
Let each student make an individual calendar using number patterns. Instruct them to write a numeral or a number sentence to match the picture for each day.

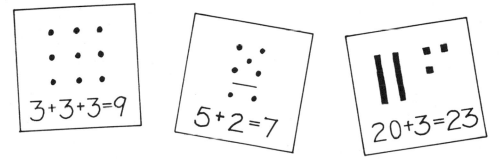

20. Number Line Puzzle (Active)

Objective: Ordering pictures and numerals 1 to 100

Grade level: 1–2

Group size: Individuals

Materials: Pictorial and numeral number line strips made from the large charts (see page 6) and two large blank charts the size of the charts (see page 7). Or, pictorial and numeral number line strips made from the small charts (pages 90–91) and two small blank charts (page 92)

Procedure: Have students make the large 1 to 100 pictorial puzzle by placing the number line strips from the large pictorial chart in order on the large blank chart. They can make the numeral puzzle in the same manner on the other large blank chart. Or, they can place the numeral number line strips over the pictorial number line strips. (Use the small number line strips in the same way on the small blank chart. If the strips have pictures glued on the back, turn the puzzle over for self-checking.

Variation 1
Use the large pictorial strips to help students make a long horizontal number line that stretches across the floor. Then students can place the large numeral strips just below the matching pictorial strips. Or, use the small number line strips in the same manner.

Variation 2
Do this as a cut-and-paste activity using different colors for the worksheets. Have students cut and paste the pictorial strips to the numeral chart. Or, cut and paste the pictorial or numeral strips to a blank chart.

21. Number Line Strips and Cards Match (Active)

Objective: Matching pictures and numerals; ordering numbers 1 to 100

Grade level: 1–3

Group size: Small group

Materials: Pictorial and numeral number line strips made from either the large charts or the small charts (see page 6) and pictorial and numeral cards made from either the large charts or the small charts (see pages 6, 7)

Procedure: Divide the group into two teams. One team makes a long horizontal number line with the large pictorial strips and matches the large numeral cards just below. The other team makes a long horizontal number line with the large numeral strips and matches the large pictorial cards just below. Or, use the small number line strips and cards in the same manner.

22. 1 to 100 Chart Match (Large charts)

Objective: Matching pictures and numerals; ordering numbers 1 to 100

Grade level: 1–3

Group size: Small group or individuals

Materials: Pictorial and numeral cards made from the large charts (see page 6), large pictorial and numeral charts, and a large blank chart (see page 7)

Procedure: At a learning center, have an individual student or small groups of students place the large pictorial cards on a large pictorial, numeral, or blank chart (or place the large numeral cards on a large pictorial, numeral, or blank chart). When the chart is completed, have players turn the cards facedown. Then they can play a game in which each player takes a turn pointing to a card, naming it, and then looking at it. If the player identifies it correctly, the player removes the card.

Variation
One or two players can use six to ten pairs of matching pictorial and numeral cards to play concentration.

23. 1 to 100 Chart Match (Small charts)

Objective: Matching pictures and numerals; ordering numbers 1 to 100

Grade level: 1–3

Group size: Whole class

Materials: Small pictorial and numeral charts (pages 90–91), pictorial and numeral cards made from the small charts (see page 7), a small blank chart (page 92); and for Variation 1, the small charts duplicated on different colors of paper

Procedure: Have students match the small pictorial cards on a small pictorial, numeral, or blank chart. Then have them match the small numeral cards on any of the three small charts. To help students associate the pictures and numerals, you may want to show the numeral transparency laid over the pictorial transparency on an overhead projector.

Variation 1
Use colored copies of the worksheets to make this a cut-and-paste activity. Tell students to cut apart the pictorial cards and paste them to the numeral chart. Then they can cut apart the pictorial or numeral cards and paste them to the blank chart.

Variation 2
If the task in this activity is too overwhelming for students, have them sort out just two rows of consecutive numbers and place the numbers in order on the blank chart. Check to see that students use the correct rows on the blank chart. Students should turn over the cards at random, one at a time, and place them correctly on the blank chart. This could be used as a "Twenty Card Race."

Variation 3
One or two players can use six to ten pairs of matching pictorial and numeral cards to play concentration.

24. Fill in the Blanks

Objective: Sequencing pictures and numerals 1 to 100

Grade level: 2–3

Group size: Whole class

Materials: Fill in the Blanks worksheets (pages 118 and 119); and for the variation, a small blank chart (page 92)

Procedure: Instruct students to draw pictures (sticks and dots) in the missing blanks on page 118 and to write numerals in the missing blanks on page 119. You may want to do a few on the overhead projector with transparencies of the worksheets so students will understand the procedure. Then you could place transparencies of the 1 to 100 charts over the transparencies of the worksheets.

Variation
Have students fill in every square on a small blank chart with either a picture or a numeral. Again, you could show transparencies of the pictorial and numeral charts placed over the blank chart.

25. Poke-and-Peek Fun

Objective: Counting tens and ones

Grade level: 1–2

Group size: Individuals

Materials: Pictorial poke-and-peek cards (see page 6)

Procedure: Have individual students work at a learning center to count the tens and ones on a card. Then show them how to poke a stick or pencil in the hole for the answer they want and to turn the card over to see if it is correct.

26. Paper Plate Match (Active)

Objective: Matching and ordering pictures and numerals 1 to 100

Grade level: 1–2

Group size: Individuals

Materials: Paper plate puzzles (see page 11)

Procedure: Have individual students work on the floor to complete each two-piece puzzle by matching the pictorial representation to the numeral. Then have them order the paper plate puzzles from smallest to largest. Students should say the numbers aloud to practice counting consecutively, counting by tens, or just reading numbers at random.

Variation
Have students order the paper plate puzzles from largest to smallest to practice counting backwards.

27. Five-Way Match (Active)

Objective: Matching pictures, tens and ones, numerals, and the expanded and word forms of numbers 1 to 100

Grade level: 2–3 (Variation 4: 1)

Group size: Whole class

Materials: Five sets of "active game" cards (see page 10)

Procedure: Scatter one set of the cards around the room faceup. Give each child about four cards from each of the other four sets. The object is to complete five-way matches all around the room.

Variation 1
Make several small sets of the matched cards for students to use at the learning center. A small set might include ten five-way matches (total of fifty cards).

Variation 2
Use all of the sets at random for a quick drill whenever five minutes are available.

Variation 3
Sort out ten matching sets (fifty cards) and have small groups play "Slap." Forty problem cards are placed facedown in the stock pile. The ten numeral cards are the answer cards and are scattered faceup around the edge of the stock pile. For each round, one player is the leader, turning over the problem cards one at a time. The remaining players try to be first to "slap," or touch, the answer card that is a match. The first player to "slap" the answer card gets the problem card. Play continues until all the problem cards have been won. The player with the most cards at the end of the game is the winner. Another child is the leader for the second round of play.

Variation 4
Play this game as a two-way match, using only two sets of cards.

28. Expanded Notation Drill

Objective: Drill for expanded notation

Grade level: 1–3

Group size: Small group or two students

Materials: Triangular expanded notation cards (see page 10)

Procedure: Use this set of cards for quick drill. When covering the top part of the card, ask, "If I put these two numbers together, what do I have?" When covering either the tens or ones part, ask, "What part of thirty-six is missing?"

29. Playing on a Giant 1 to 100 Chart (Active)

Objective: Practice with numbers 1 to 100

Grade level: 2–3

Group size: Whole class

Materials: Giant 1 to 100 chart and giant blank chart (see page 10), double spinners (pages 109–112), sets of pictorial and numeral cards made from the large charts (see page 6), two bean bags, small pictorial charts (page 90), acetate, crayons and wipes, and place value mats (page 103)

Procedure: Place the giant 1 to 100 chart in the middle of the room. Give each student a small pictorial chart and have them sit around the edge of the giant chart. Students take turns spinning and reading one of the four spinners. The player designated as "it" walks to stand on the numeral called. The other children use their small pictorial charts and "let their fingers do the walking." "It" gets three turns and then another player does the walking. Then have the students walk by twos or threes, starting at the number spun and counting the sequence aloud as the other students "walk" with their fingers on their charts.

Variation 1
Place the giant 1 to 100 chart in the middle of the room. Toss the bean bag onto the chart. Then tell students to draw a picture of that number and record the numeral on their place value mats covered with acetate.

Variation 2
Place the giant 1 to 100 chart in the middle of the room. Divide the class into two teams. Someone from the first team spins a number, reads it, and then tries to toss the bean bag to that number on the chart. The team gets three points if the player tosses the bean bag in the middle of that square, one point if the bean bag touches one of the border lines, and no points if the bean bag does not touch the square at all. Teams alternate play and keep score. You can also play this game with the giant blank chart. Team members take turns tossing the bean bag onto the chart. The team gets one point if the player gives the number name, two points if the player gives the meaning in tens and ones, and three points if the player gives the expanded notation form.

Variation 3
Place the giant blank chart in the middle of the room and choose three students to walk on the chart. Have the other students sit around the chart and distribute all of the large pictorial cards to them. As music plays, the three students walk slowly and softly on the blank chart. When the music stops, they stop in one

of the squares. Each student who has a picture card that matches the spot where one of the three children stopped gets to place that pictorial card in the square and trade places with the walker. Once a card is placed in a square, players can no longer walk in it. The game continues until the chart is full of picture cards. You can also play this game using the large numeral cards.

30. Walking on a Giant 1 to 100 Chart (Active)

Objective: Practice in following directions

Grade level: 2–3

Group size: Small group

Materials: Giant 1 to 100 chart (see page 10)

Procedure: Take a small group of students into the hall or the gym. Place the giant 1 to 100 numeral chart in the middle of the floor. Then give directions for a student to follow. The student should listen carefully, wait two seconds, follow the instructions, and then tell the ending number. Tell the student to face the top of the chart at all times. Examples of instructions:

1. Start at 37, (pause) go left 2, up 1, right 4. (29)
2. Start at 100, (pause) go up 4, left 2, down 1. (68)
3. Start at 54, (pause) 10 more, 2 more. (66)
4. Start at 11, (pause) 1 less, 2 tens more. (30)
5. Start at 85, (pause) go north 2, east 4, south 3. (99)
6. Start at 51, (pause) 2 more tens, 4 more ones. (75)

Refer to Arrow Math, Activities 71, 72, and 73, which are also fun for walking on the giant chart.

31. Egg Carton Toss (Active)

Objective: Understanding numbers 1 to 100 and odd and even; counting by fives

Grade level: 2–3

Group size: Small group

Materials: Ten ten-cartons (see page 9), game markers, small numeral chart (page 91), pencil, and paper

Procedure: Arrange the 10 ten-cartons to form a 10×10 flat. Give each player 10 to 15 of a different color of game markers. Then have players take turns tossing a marker into one of the egg holes. If a player can tell what number corresponds to that egg hole, he or she gets two points; if the player can give the expanded notation sentence, he or she gets two more points. After ten tosses for each player, the one with the most points is the winner.

Variation 1
Place the 10 ten-cartons in columns to form the 10×10 flat. This way it becomes obvious where the odd and even numbers are located. (Review Activity 7 if needed.) Players take turns tossing one of their markers into an egg hole. If the toss is an odd number, the ones digit is the score; if the toss is an even number, the tens digit is the score. The first player to reach 100 is the winner.

Variation 2
Arrange the 10 ten-cartons in rows so it is easy to locate the multiples of 5. Players take turns tossing one of their chips into an egg hole. Players earn that

number of points only when it is a multiple of 5. The player who reaches 300 first is the winner. You will need to clarify rules about where to stand for each toss.

32. Catcher's Mitt Math (Active)

Objective: Recognition of pictures and numerals 1 to 100

Grade level: 1–2

Group size: Whole class

Materials: Large pictorial and numeral charts displayed where students can see them, set of pictorial and numeral cards made from the large charts (see page 6), several catcher's mitts (see page 7); and for the variations, number line strips (see page 6), and a large blank chart (see page 7)

Procedure: "Today we will play catch with numbers." Draw a pictorial card and "throw" it to a student by saying it aloud; for example "2 tens and 5 ones." A student "catches" the number by moving the mitt to the correct picture on the large pictorial chart. Draw a numeral card and "throw" that number to the same student. This time the student "catches" the number by moving the mitt on the large numeral chart until the correct numeral is showing through the hole. Throw each player three numbers, and then give someone else a chance. Try "throwing" the picture and having students "catch" the numeral—or just the reverse.

Variation 1
Do this same activity on the number line strips rather than the large charts.

Variation 2
Use a large blank chart for students to point to the number that you "throw." They are "catching" with the pointer rather than the mitt.

Variation 3
Point to a picture or numeral on one of the large charts or number line strips. The student should quickly give you the name for the picture of that number. Then try pointing to a number and having students respond with the number before, after, above, or below.

33. Cover Your Chart

Objective: Recognition of pictures and numerals 1 to 100; practice with tens and ones

Grade level: 1–2

Group size: Whole class

Materials: Small pictorial and numeral charts (pages 90–91) and game markers

Procedure: Give each student a small pictorial chart. Call out a number and tell students to use a marker to cover the picture of that number as quickly as possible. Continue in this same way as long as necessary for students to gain familiarity with the 1 to 100 pictorial chart. Next have students use the numeral chart. Call out the meaning (for example, "4 tens, 6 ones" or "9 ones, 7 tens") and tell students to cover the numeral as quickly as possible. Be sure to say the ones first part of the time and the tens first part of the time to help students work on good listening. Continue until students grasp the meaning of numbers from 1 to 100.

34. Jigsaw Game

Objective: Recognition of pictures and numerals 1 to 100

Grade level: 2–3

Group size: Whole class or small group

Materials: Small pictorial, numeral, or blank charts (pages 90–92) and crayons; and for the variation, a large numeral or blank chart and cards made from the large pictorial chart (see pages 6–7)

Procedure: Give each student a pictorial, numeral, or blank chart according to their skill level. Before the game begins, have each student enclose eight contiguous boxes somewhere on the chart. Call out the meaning of a number (for example, "4 tens, 2 ones") or the expanded form ("40 plus 2") and cover it on your master chart. When you call one of the numbers in a student's configuration of eight boxes, that student can color in the number, picture, or blank space. The first student to color his or her configuration completely is the winner. On the same charts, have students enclose eight different boxes, use a different color, and play the game again. Clear the master chart between games so you can verify the winners from the master chart.

Variation

Play this game on the large numeral or blank chart with a small group. Have each student enclose a ten-box configuration that does not overlap anyone else's. Place the large pictorial cards in a box. Players take turns drawing a card. If the card can be played in that player's configuration, it is placed on the playing board. If the card cannot be played, it is returned to the drawing box and the next player takes a turn. The first player to fill his or her configuration completely is the winner.

35. Listen and Do

Objective: Practice in following directions

Grade level: 1–3

Group size: Small group

Materials: Small numeral charts (page 91), acetate sheets, and crayons and wipes

Procedure: Ask students to listen as you give them two-, three-, or four-step directions. Then after a few seconds of silence, say, "Go." The students should follow the directions. Check their work, have them clean off the charts, and then give them another set of directions. Here are a few suggestions for directions:

1. Put a blue X on 99. Circle 22 with red.
2. Draw a green line from 54 to 84, box in 2 with yellow.
3. Put a yellow X on every number with a zero, circle 62 with purple.

36. Call a Number

Objective: Writing numerals for tens and ones

Grade level: 1–2

Group size: Whole class

Materials: Large blank chart (see page 7) displayed where students can see it, wipe-off pen or crayon, and wipe

Procedure: Say something like "I am thinking of a number that has 2 tens and 3 ones." Ask if anyone knows where that number should be written on the chart and have them write it in the proper place. If correct, this person becomes the leader, saying something like, "I am thinking of a number that has 5 ones and 8 tens." Continue the game as long as needed for practice. You may want to complete the chart over a period of several days.

Variation

Use this same idea with two teams. Each team uses a different color of crayon, and has one team member act as the recorder. Team players alternate giving the number meaning while the recorder fills in that numeral on the chart in the team color. Each team tries to get four in a row first—vertically, horizontally, or diagonally. Once a numeral is filled in on the chart, it cannot be given again.

37.   More and Less Fun

Objective: Familiarity with ten more, ten less, one more, one less

Grade level: 1–3

Group size: Two students

Materials: Small pictorial or numeral chart (pages 90–91), game markers for each player, one of the double spinners (pages 109–112), and the more or less spinner (page 113)

Procedure: Each player spins one of the double spinners to see where on the chart to place a marker for "Start." Set aside the double spinner. Players than take turns spinning the more or less spinner to determine each move. Play continues until one player goes off the playing board. Familiarity with ten less, ten more, one less, and one more on the chart is very important. This is a quick game for that concept that students can play several times.

38.   Three in a Row

Objective: Recognition of pictures and numerals 1 to 100; practice with tens and ones

Grade level: 1–2

Group size: Small group

Materials: Large pictorial, numeral, or blank chart, pictorial and numeral cards made from the large charts (see page 6), one of the double spinners (pages 109–112), the more or less spinner (page 113), small pictorial or numeral charts (pages 90–91), game markers, small blank charts (page 92), and crayons and wipes

Procedure: Note that this game can also be played as "four in a row" or "five in a row." Each player begins with a small pictorial chart and game markers. Players take turns drawing a large pictorial card, reading it, and covering the picture for that number with a marker on their chart. Play continues around the small group. The first person to get three in a row is the winner. Now try using the numeral cards with the pictorial chart. Mix the cards and charts for each game for appropriate practice. Students may prefer to play this game using a large chart as the playing board. In this case, each player uses a different color of markers.

Variation 1

Give each student a small blank chart. Each player selects a card and records the picture or numeral on the blank chart. Three in a row wins. If you use the large blank chart as the playing board for the whole group, each player would use a different color crayon to record their numbers.

Variation 2

Use the large pictorial or numeral chart as the playing board and the single more or less spinner. Each player uses a different color of game markers. Players take turns drawing a large pictorial or numeral card *and* spinning the spinner. Using the card number and the amount spun, the player computes the number and covers it with a marker on the playing board. If the space is already covered, the player draws and spins again. Three in a row wins.

Variation 3

Use the large pictorial or numeral chart as the playing board and one of the double spinners. Each player needs ten game markers of a different color. Players take turns spinning one of the spinners to determine the number they should cover for that turn. If a player spins a number that is already covered, the player places the marker for that turn *on top* of the other player's marker. Play continues until all the players have placed all their chips on the playing board. The player with the most chips *showing on top* is the winner.

39.   1 to 100 Chart Bingo

Objective: Practice with numbers 1 to 100

Grade level: 2–3

Group size: Whole class

Materials: Small numeral chart (page 91), small blank charts (page 92), and game markers

Procedure: First have students make individual bingo cards by filling in the numerals on the blank charts as follows: Write the numbers 1 to 10 at random in the first row; write the numbers 11 to 20 at random in the second row; write the numbers 21 to 30 at random in the third row, and so on until the chart has numerals written in every space. Because each row is a decade of numbers, students get practice in finding the eighty row, the fifty row, and so on. Finding the "called" number in the row should not be hard. Use the small numeral chart as the master to keep track of numbers called. The first player to get ten in a row—vertically, horizontally, or diagonally—is the winner. The winner calls out the numbers covered to verify that they have been called. When players use game markers, this game can be played several times. Friends may want to trade their bingo cards. Possible calls include: "Place a marker on 47, … on the number that comes after 49, … on the number that comes before 81, … on the number that is one more than 26, … on the number that is ten less than 18, … on the number that is ten more than 72, … on the number that is five less than 60, … 4 tens 6 ones," and so on. You could also include problems for computational skills, word problems, money questions, and general information such as days in March, eggs in a dozen, months in the year, inches in a foot, or the date of a holiday. The amount of time it takes you to write out one, two, or three calls for each number on the chart is well spent, because the list can be used over and over. Keep the cards for the next time you play bingo.

40. Tens and Ones Review

Objective: Review of pictures and numerals for tens and ones

Grade level: 2–3

Group size: Whole class

Materials: Base ten materials (see pages 9–10) available at a learning center, copies of the Tens and Ones Review worksheet on page 124, and small 1 to 100 charts for reference

Procedure: Students should fill in the boxes on the worksheet with pictures *and* numerals. The 10 less, 1 less, 1 greater, and 10 greater should always be applied to the number in the center column. Students who still need manipulatives to complete this activity should be encouraged to use the learning center. Have the pictorial and numeral charts available for reference. Repeat Activity 37 if necessary.

41. More Tens and Ones Review

Objective: Review of tens and ones and expanded notation

Grade level: 2–3

Group size: Whole class

Materials: Base ten materials (see page 9) and expanded notation cards (page 8) available at a learning center and copies of the Tens and Ones Review worksheets on pages 125–126

Procedure: Tell students to fill in the blanks. These worksheets require careful thinking and a complete understanding of tens and ones, including the expanded notation form. Thus you should use them only for a final review and check. Complete the first few with the class to be sure they understand what they are being asked to do. Students who still need manipulatives and expanded notation cards to complete this activity should be encouraged to use the learning center.

42. Find Your Partner (Active)

Objective: Matching pictures and numerals 1 to 100; ordering numbers 1 to 100

Grade level: 1–2

Group size: Whole class

Materials: Matching sets of pictorial and numeral cards made from the large charts (see page 6) that total the class size. (If the class size is 28, you will need 14 matching sets, or 28 cards: 1–14, 25–38, 57–70, 87–100, or 14 random sets.)

Procedure: Play this visual game in silence. Mix the numeral and pictorial cards in a box. Each player draws one card. When you say "Go," students race to find their partner. When two partners find each other, they find their proper place in the line at the front of the room. Time the class to see how long it takes to get all the pairs in order from smallest to largest. Try it again and see if the class can beat its original time.

Variation
Make one extra "Poison card" for each set of cards and play "Old Maid" in small groups. Deal all the cards. The object is to make as many matches as

possible. Players take turns drawing a card from the previous player and setting aside any matches. The game ends when one player is out of cards. Two points are scored for each match, five points subtracted for the Poison card. Play five rounds and determine a winner.

43. Know Your Neighbor (Active)

Objective:	Ordering numbers 1 to 100
Grade level:	1–3
Group size:	Whole class
Materials:	Five sets of "active game" cards (see page 10); use only one set at a time
Procedure:	Pass each player three or four cards until you pass out one whole set. Choose one player to start the game. That player brings a card to the front of the class and says, for example, "I am 51; who are my neighbors?" The player who has 50 comes up and says, "I am 50; I live before 51" (or "I am 50; I am one less than 51"). The player who has 52 also comes up and says, "I am 52; I live after 51" (or "I am 52; I am one more than 51"). The three players stand in front, holding the numbers so all can see. Then choose another player to start another round of the game.

Variation 1
Have players try to build a ten-car train of neighbors.

Variation 2
Have neighbors above and below the first number come to the front as well. Have the five players stand on marked places on the floor, if necessary.

44. Smaller or Larger Numbers

Objective:	Sorting and ordering numbers 1 to 100
Grade level:	1–2 (Variation: 3–4)
Group size:	Whole class
Materials:	Sets of pictorial and numeral cards made from the small charts (see page 7) and a piece of paper divided down the center. (Have students make a place for a "target" card at the top of the paper and write *smaller* on the left side and *larger* on the right side, as shown below.)

smaller	target	larger

Procedure:	Place a target card at the top center of the paper. Have students sort all the cards by placing them on either the left or the right side according to their relationship to the target card. Students can have a neighbor check their work. Ask students, "If you know the target card, can you predict how many cards

will end up on each side of the paper?" (Example: if the target card is 49, 48 cards will end up on the left side, and 51 on the right side.)

Variation
For third and fourth graders, have them place the target card at the top and then estimate how many of the next ten cards might be placed on each side. Talk about ratios and percentages.

45. Jigsaw Puzzles

Objective: Ordering pictures and numerals 1 to 100

Grade level: 2–3

Group size: Individuals

Materials: Pictorial and numeral jigsaw puzzles made from the small charts (see page 8) and small pictorial and numeral charts (pages 90–91) for reference

Procedure: Have students work at a learning center to put the puzzle pieces together to complete small pictorial and numeral charts. When they are working on the puzzles, have the small charts available for a visual guide. If the puzzles were made with pictures on the back, have students complete the puzzle on a book or hard board so that a second book or hard surface can be used to turn the puzzle over for self-checking.

46. Jigsaw Pieces

Objective: Practice with 1 to 100 chart segments

Grade level: 2–4

Group size: Whole class

Materials: Copies of the chart segments worksheets on pages 120–123 and small pictorial and numeral charts (pages 90–91) available for reference

Procedure: The worksheets contain puzzle pieces from 1 to 100 charts. Each piece is only a small part of the 1 to 100 chart, but it has a clue given. Tell students to draw pictures (sticks and dots) in the blanks on worksheets from pages 120–121 and to write numerals in the blanks on worksheets from pages 122 and 123. Have the small pictorial and numeral charts (pages 90–91) available if needed.

47. Geoboard Puzzle

Objective: Ordering numbers 1 to 100

Grade level: 2–3

Group size: Individuals

Materials: 10 × 10 geoboard and plastic bread bag fasteners labeled 1 to 100 (see page 11) and small pictorial and numeral charts (pages 90–91) for reference

Procedure: Students should place the plastic fasteners over the geoboard nails in order from 1 to 100. Have a 1 to 100 chart available for reference and checking. Students should pick a numbered bread fastener at random and place it on the geoboard in the correct place before they pick another fastener. Discourage students from hunting for numbers in consecutive order.

48. Window Pane Math (Active)

Objective: Practice with numbers 1 to 100

Grade level: 2–4

Group size: Whole class

Materials: Large pictorial and numeral charts displayed where students can see them and several posterboard window frames (see page 7)

Procedure: Each student takes a turn positioning the window frame so that a picture or numeral shows in the open pane. Have the student say what number comes before, after, above, and below that picture or numeral. With older students, include the diagonals. Students should be able to give the name and meaning in tens and ones for any pane in the 5 × 5 window frame.

49. Numbers in Order

Objective: Ordering pictures and numbers 1 to 100

Grade level: 2–3

Group size: Whole class, working in pairs (or threes)

Materials: Small pictorial and numeral charts (pages 90–91), pictorial and numeral cards made from the small charts (see page 7), and game markers

Procedure: Use both the pictorial and numeral cards, separately or mixed. Turn the cards facedown. One student draws five cards and orders them smallest to largest. Then the partner verifies the order by using markers to cover each picture or numeral on the small pictorial and numeral charts. For the next round, students should reverse roles.

Variation

Students can play "Middle Wins" with three players. Each player draws two cards, decides which card to keep, and discards the other one without letting the other players know what was kept. Then each player puts down the card he or she kept. The players order the three cards, and the player whose card is in the middle of the sequence gets a point. The first player to get five points is the winner.

50. In Order (I)

Objective: Ordering numbers 1 to 100

Grade level: 2–3

Group size: Whole class

Materials: Set of the numeral cards made from the large chart (see page 6) or one of the double spinners (pages 109–112), pencil, and paper

Procedure: Have each student draw a row of three boxes on his or her paper. Draw a card *or* spin a spinner and call the number. Instruct students to write the number in any one of the three boxes. Call another number and have students write it in one of the remaining two boxes on their paper. Then call a third number and have students place it in the last empty box. Each student who has the three numbers in order from smallest to largest gets a point. Play continues until someone has ten points.

Variation 1
Increase the number of boxes to four, five, or six.

Variation 2
In a small group, each student should make a playing board with six to eight boxes. Players take turns drawing a pictorial or numeral card and placing it in one of the boxes where it seems the most appropriate for ordering. Cards cannot be moved once they are placed on the grid. The object of the game is to create an ordered sequence. If a player draws a card that cannot be placed in order, that player is out of the game. The player who completes an ordered sequence or stays in the game the longest is the winner.

51. In Order (II)

Objective: Ordering pictures and numbers 1 to 100; experience in problem solving

Grade level: 2–4

Group size: Whole class

Materials: Pictorial or numeral cards made from the small charts (see page 7), paper, and pencil

Procedure: To play this solitaire game, a player draws a 3 × 4 grid, with spaces large enough to hold one of the cards, on a piece of paper. The object is to fill the grid with cards in order from smallest to largest in a left to right sequence. The cards are mixed and placed facedown. The player draws one card at a time and places it where it seems most appropriate for ordering. Once a card is placed down, it cannot be moved. If the player draws a card that cannot be placed in order on the grid, the game is over. Students can play this game again and again, trying to complete the grid in sequence using the first twelve cards drawn. Students can play individually or in pairs with one player acting as the judge to see if the other player orders the cards correctly. Challenge students to see how many times they can complete the grid. It is hard; keep trying!

Variation
The large cards could be used at a learning center with a 3 × 4 playing grid. Or, have students try using a 3 × 5 grid and drawing fifteen cards.

52. Ordering Numbers Relay (Active)

Objective: Ordering numbers 1 to 100

Grade level: 2–3

Group size: Whole class, divided into two teams

Materials: One set of "active game" cards (see page 10) divided equally between the teams

Procedure: Place two piles of cards on a small desk next to the middle of the chalkboard tray. Stand near by to act as the judge. When you say "Go," the first player of each team runs to the team pile, picks up three cards, and orders them from the smallest to largest in the chalkboard tray. When the judge taps the shoulder of a player because his or her cards are ordered correctly, the player runs back to the line and tags the next player on the team, who repeats the procedure, stacking the set of three cards in front of the previous three. The team that orders all of the team cards first is the winner.

Variation
Mix cards from all five sets to use for ordering.

53. Sequence Game (I)

Objective: Ordering numbers 1 to 100

Grade level: 2–3

Group size: Small group

Materials: Pictorial or numeral cards made from the large charts (see page 6) and card holders (see page 7) if available

Procedure: The object of the game is to order the pictorial or numeral cards from smallest to largest in a left to right sequence. Deal each player five cards faceup. Players arrange their cards in a row (or in the card holder) starting at the left, in the order that they were dealt. Then they place the remaining cards facedown in a stack and start a discard pile by placing one card faceup next to it. The first player either draws a card or picks up the discard. If the card picked up will assist the order of the player's cards, the player can discard a dealt card and replace it with the drawn card. The new card must go in the same position as the discarded card. If the drawn card does not improve a player's order, the player can discard it faceup on the discard pile. Play continues in this manner until a player has successfully ordered five cards from smallest to largest in a left to right sequence.

Variation

The object of this game is to create a pictorial or numeral train. Deal each player five cards, which they can hold in their hand or place in the card holder. (It is wise for players to order the cards from the smallest to largest.) The first player places a card in the center of the table. The next player adds a card whose pictorial or numeral value is smaller or larger than the first card, placing a card with lesser value to the left of the initial card and a card with greater value to the right of the initial card. Play continues as each player tries to add a card at either the smaller or larger end of the "train." Players cannot place cards between the cards in the train. When a player cannot add a card to either end of the train, the player drops out of the game. Play continues until one player has placed all five cards in the train or until none of the players can add a card to it. At the end of the game, the player without cards or the player with the least number of cards is the winner.

54. Sequence Game (II)

Objective: Sequencing numbers 1 to 100; experience with number patterns

Grade level: 2–4

Group size: Small group

Materials: Numeral cards made from the large chart (see page 6), card holders (see page 7) if available, and pencil and paper if keeping score

Procedure: The object of the game is to get three sets of three cards in consecutive order. Each player draws ten cards. The rest of the cards go facedown in a stock pile. Turn the top card over to begin a discard pile. The first player can draw a card from the stock pile or pick up one from the discard pile. When a player has three sets of three cards in consecutive order, that player is the winner. If students want to keep score, start by giving each player ten points. If the winning card comes from the stock pile, everyone forfeits one point to the winner. If the winning card comes from the discard pile, the player who discarded the card forfeits two points. The first player to reach twenty points is the winner.

Variation
Extend the object of the game to allow the three ordered cards to be in a pattern like 49, 59, 69; 10, 20, 30; or 3, 5, 7.

55. Sign Fun

Objective:	Familiarity with equality and inequality number sentences
Grade level:	1–3
Group size:	Individuals
Materials:	Pictorial and numeral cards made from the large charts (see page 6) and the large sign circles (page 101)
Procedure:	Discuss equality, inequality, and how relational symbols ($=\neq><$) are used with numerals to convey a complete mathematical idea. Use the twelve signs and the pictorial and numeral cards to have students make twelve complete sentences. Have them record the picture and numeral sentences on paper.

56. Building Odd and Even

Objective:	Understanding of odd and even and counting by twos
Grade level:	1–3
Group size:	Whole class
Materials:	Ten-frames, some not glued to tagboard (see page 9) and loose beans (with young children, the ten-cartons [see page 9] work well with multilinks for teaching odd and even because they are easier to handle); game markers, crayons, small numeral charts (page 91); and for Variation 2, multilinks
Procedure:	Refer to Activity 7, which teaches odd and even using ten-frames. Have students begin to build consecutive numbers in the ten-frames. Whenever they build an even number, place a marker over that number on your master numeral chart. After they reach 40, ask students to cover the rest of the even numbers on the chart without building them. Ask, "What is the pattern?" (odd and even alternate) "Count the numbers covered." (counting by twos) "Look at the ones digits in each row—what is repeated?" (2, 4, 6, 8, 0) "How many odd numbers and how many even numbers are on the chart?" (50 of each) "What can you say about each column of numbers?" (all the numbers in a given column are either odd or even)

Variation 1
On a small numeral chart, have students color in the odd/even pattern using two colors. Then have them practice counting on by twos from any given number.

Variation 2
Have students use two colors of multilinks to build a tower in which the colors alternate. Then tell them to break off four multilinks from the tower and place them flat as the first row. They should continue to break off groups of four multilinks and to place them below one another in rows. Ask, "What pattern do you see?" (The same colors are in columns.) Then tell them to break off

sets of five multilinks from the tower and place them in rows. Ask, "What pattern do you see this time?" (The colors are in a checkerboard pattern.) Have them try six in a row, then seven in a row. Ask, "Can you draw some conclusions or make some predictions?" Students could color these patterns on 4 × 4, 5 × 5, 6 × 6, and 7 × 7 grids using crayons of two colors. Discuss why the pattern is either in columns or checkered. In this activity, students are learning about odds and evens unconsciously.

57. Odd/Even Climb

Objective: Experience with odd and even

Grade level: 2–3

Group size: Two players

Materials: Pictorial and numeral cards made from the large or small charts (see pages 6, 7), playing boards drawn on paper as shown below; and for the variation, poke-and-peek odd/even cards (see page 6)

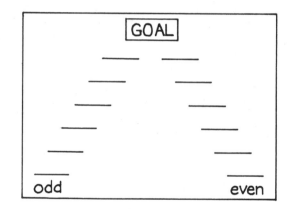

Procedure: One player is "odd" and climbs the left side of the board; the other player is "even" and climbs the right side of the board. The object is to reach the top of the board first. Players take turns drawing a card and either placing it on their side of the board or discarding it. If, for example, the "odd" player draws an odd card, he or she can place it on the next line on the left side of the board; if the "odd" player draws an even card, the card is discarded. Play continues until one player reaches the top. Switch roles for the second game.

Variation
Use the poke-and-peek odd/even cards for a quick review.

58. Cards That Teach

Objective: Experience in sorting and problem solving

Grade level: 2–3

Group size: Whole class

Materials: Pictorial and numeral cards made from the small charts (see page 7)

Procedure: Begin this activity by sorting students into two groups (for example, those with blue eyes and those with another color eyes; those wearing red and those not wearing red; or those wearing pants and those in skirts). Then sort some students into groups by just telling them in which group to stand. Ask the class to guess what you are using for sorting attributes. Next work with students to sort the pictorial cards into two piles, letting students come up with their own ideas. Here are a few suggestions to get them started: pictures with 5 or more tens and pictures with fewer than 5 tens; pictures with 5 or more ones and pictures with fewer than 5 ones; pictures with and without the same number of tens and ones; or pictures with an even number of tens and pictures with an uneven number of tens. Then have students sort numeral cards into two piles. A few suggestions: numbers with and without a 3 in the ones place; numbers with and without a 7 as one of the digits; numbers you make using only straight lines (1, 4, 7) and numbers you make using curved lines; even numbers and odd numbers; or numbers divisible by 5 and numbers not divisible by 5.

Variation

Have students play "Read My Mind" with a friend. One player begins to sort the cards in a particular way while the other player observes in silence. When the second player thinks he or she has determined the rule, that player takes over the sorting. The first player observes the other's sorting to confirm that the other player has determined the rule or to take back the cards and continue sorting until the other player can determine the rule correctly. This game requires keen observation and should be played in silence.

59. Winning Rules

Objective: Experience in sorting and problem solving

Grade level: 2–3

Group size: Small group

Materials: Large blank chart (see page 7) and pictorial and numeral cards made from the large charts (see page 6)

Procedure: Deal all of the pictorial or numeral cards to the players. Players take turns giving rules for placing cards on the large blank chart. The first player might say, "All numbers with a 6 as a digit." Then all players get to place their cards that match the rule on the chart. Then the next player states a rule such as, "All numbers with 4 tens" or "All numbers less than 15" or "odd numbers." The first player to get rid of all of his or her cards is the winner. When students have completed the chart, have them play the game in reverse by removing cards. A player states a rule and collects those cards that match the rule. At the end, the player with the fewest cards is the winner.

60. Twenty-One

Objective: Experience in problem solving

Grade level: 2–4

Group size: Whole class playing in pairs

Materials: Small numeral charts (page 91), acetate, and two colors of game markers, or crayons and wipes

Procedure: This game can be played by two students when they have a little time. They can play orally or by crossing out (or covering) numbers on the numeral chart. The object of the game is to *not* be the player who has to say or cross out 21. Players alternate crossing out one or two consecutive numbers, progressing from

1 to 21. For example, the first player can cover 1 or 1, 2. Play continues until one player covers 21 and loses the game. Have students play this game often. When do students begin to notice key numbers (numbers that a player needs to cross out to control the game)? After 20, they usually notice 17 as a key number, then 14 and 11. Ask, "Do you notice a pattern? Why are those key numbers?" Over weeks or months, allow students to enjoy this game and develop their own winning strategies.

Variation
Change the roles for winning and losing. That is, have the winner be the player who says the last number. You could also allow each player to cross out one, two, or three numbers for each turn.

61. Twenty Questions

Objective: Experience in problem solving

Grade level: 3–4

Group size: Whole class

Materials: Numeral cards made from the large chart (see page 6), small numeral charts (page 91), acetate, and crayons and wipes

Procedure: Choose one student to be the leader. The leader draws a target card and does not tell the other players what the number is. The other players then ask questions to help them determine the number. Is it an even number? Is it less than 50? Does it have 5 as a digit? Does it have 3 tens? They are allowed twenty questions but only one greater than/less than question per game. The leader keeps track of the number of questions they ask. The goal is to ask the fewest number of questions to get to the target number. As they ask questions, players can cross out numbers on their numeral chart to help them zero in on the target number. Choose a new leader for each game. Encourage older students to include questions about multiples, factors, prime numbers, and composites.

62. Battleship

Objective: Practice with expanded notation; experience in problem solving

Grade level: 3–4

Group size: Two players

Materials: Two small numeral charts (page 91) for each player, acetate sheets, crayons and wipes, 3½″ × ½″ strips of paper ("battleships" that each cover four numbers on the small numeral charts), a cardboard divider for between players

Procedure: Have students play this game with a friend. The two players each hide four battleships on one of their numeral charts placed under an acetate sheet. The battleships may be placed either horizontally or vertically over four numerals. Each player also places another numeral chart under an acetate sheet to record hits and misses. One student begins by calling out a number in expanded form, "Twenty and three, 23." If that number is not part of any of the other player's battleship strips, the other player says, "Miss." If that number is a part of one of the battleship strips, the other player responds, "Hit." The player who called the number marks it on his or her recording numeral chart to ensure not calling it again. Each student will work out a system for marking hits and misses. Players take turns calling expanded numbers and recording hits or misses. The game is over when one player has sunk all the opponent's battleships.

63. Closest to a Tens Number

Objective: Understanding of rounding to the nearest ten

Grade level: 3–4

Group size: Whole class, playing in pairs

Materials: Small pictorial and numeral charts (pages 90–91), pictorial and numeral cards made from the small charts (see page 7) or one of the double spinners (pages 109–112), and game markers (six of one color for each player)

Procedure: Discuss with the class what it means to round to the nearest ten. Have the class look at the pictorial chart and see how the ones configurations can help decide how to round a number to the next ten. Players take turns drawing a small pictorial card. The player decides which ten the number is nearest and places a marker on that decade number. If the number is already covered, the player places the marker on top of the other one. After six rounds of play, the player with the most chips showing is the winner.

Variation
Play the game the same way, but use the numeral chart as a playing board. Draw from the set of small numeral cards, or use one of the double spinners.

5

Addition and Subtraction Activities

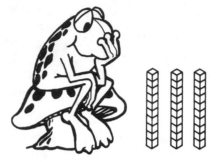

It is important to provide students many experiences in addition and subtraction—putting objects into sets, taking away objects from sets, and comparing sets. Then draw these mathematical ideas as pictures and express them as mathematical sentences using written symbols. Learning the number patterns suggested in Activity 3 helps students learn to add and subtract without counting every dot or object. They learn to count on, and eventually they know combinations from visual imagery. Adding and subtracting with or without regrouping follows naturally when students understand place value thoroughly. That is why we urge you to spend so much time on the prerequisite and place value activities. You will see the payoff when you teach all other mathematical concepts. In this section, you will find many activities for teaching addition and subtraction with the pictorial and numeral 1 to 100 charts.

64. Exploring the Charts

Objective: Seeing patterns and relationships on a 1 to 100 chart

Grade level: 3–4

Group size: Whole class

Materials: Small pictorial and numeral charts (pages 90–91) and game markers

Procedure: Explore and discuss the charts further with students, encouraging them to look for patterns. First use the pictorial chart with markers. After looking at a pattern, clear the chart of markers before discussing the next pattern. A few suggestions:

1. Cover any row. What's the difference between each picture? (one more cube)
2. Cover any column. What's the difference between each picture? (one ten-stick)

3. Cover any diagonal slanted to the left. What's the difference between each picture? (one more ten-stick and one more cube, or 10 + 1) Which of these diagonals has the same number of tens and ones? (twin digits on the numeral chart: 11, 22, 33, ...)
4. Cover any diagonal slanted to the right. What's the difference between each picture? (one more ten-stick and one less cube, or 10 − 1)
5. Cover all the pictures that have three ten-sticks. What row is it? (thirties) Cover all the pictures with eight ten-sticks. What row is it? (eighties) Point to the forties row; the nineties row; and so on.
6. Find the column that has four cubes; six cubes; no cubes; and so on.

Now use the numeral chart to have students look for those same patterns. Go back and ask some of the same questions. Here are some more suggestions:

7. Cover all the numbers that have 3 as one of its digits with one color of marker. Now cover all the numbers that have 7 as one of its digits with another color. Name the numbers that are the union of the two sets (all of the covered numbers). Name the numbers that are the intersection of the two sets (common to both sets). (37, 73) Then give students the following statements and have them observe and explain the pattern for each one (some patterns don't apply for the decade numbers).
8. Add the digits of the numbers in any row. (consecutive numbers; while the tens digit remains constant, the ones digit increases by one in each square)
9. Add the digits of the numbers in any column. (consecutive numbers; the tens digit is constant, the ones digit increases by one)
10. Add the digits of the numbers on any diagonal slanted to the right. (equal sums; the ones digit increases by one and the tens digit decreases by one)
11. Add the digits of the numbers on any diagonal slanted to the left. (counting by twos; both ones and tens digits increase by one)
12. Find the difference between the digits of the numbers in any row. (consecutive numbers in either direction from the multiple of 11; the tens digit is constant)
13. Find the difference between the digits of the numbers in any column. (consecutive numbers in either direction from the multiple of 11; the ones digit is constant)
14. Find the difference between the digits of the numbers on any diagonal slanted to the right. (counting by twos in either direction from the multiple of 11 or, in alternate diagonals, from the numbers with reversed digits—like 56 and 65; as one digit increases by one, the other decreases by one, so the difference between them varies by 2)
15. Find the difference between the digits of the numbers on any diagonal slanted to the left. (the differences are the same; both digits increase by one, so the difference remains constant)

See Activities 79, 80, and 81 to further explore patterns on the 1 to 100 charts with addition.

65. Add and Subtract Using Patterns

Objective: Ability to add and subtract without counting; understanding of mathematical sentences

Grade level: 1–2

Group size: Whole class (Variation 2: individuals)

Materials: 3 × 6 and 5 × 2 grids (page 93), game markers in two colors; and for Variation 2, dominoes

Procedure: Students learn combinations unconsciously by recognizing the pattern as one or more sets. You may want to do the activity on an overhead projector while students do the activity at their desks. Use the 3 × 6 double domino grid and the modified domino pattern (see Activity 3), because markers do not change position when they are added one at a time. Build one addend in one color of markers. Then build the second addend in the other color. Students can recognize the answer without counting when the pattern is familiar to them. Have a student say the sentence aloud (for example, "four plus three equals seven"). For subtraction, build the first number in one color of markers and then place the number of markers of the other color for the number to be subtracted on top of the chips already down. It will be obvious how many more in the first number than in the second number. Again, have the students say the sentence aloud (for example, "seven compared to three is four more").

Variation 1
Try this same activity with the ten-frame (5 × 2) grid.

Variation 2
Have students use dominoes at a learning center adding and subtracting the dots on each half of a domino. Have them write plus and minus sentences for each domino. (5 dots plus 1 dot is 6 dots; 5 + 1 = 6. 5 dots compared to 1 dot is 4 more dots; 5 − 1 = 4.)

Students can also write complete fact families for each domino, and the commutative property of addition can easily be illustrated. After they see on one of the 6 dominoes that 5 dots plus 1 dot is 6 dots, have them turn the domino around to see that 1 dot plus 5 dots is 6 dots. Then use the same domino to help students start with the total of 6 dots and take away 1 dot to have 5 left; then start with 6 dots and take away 5 dots to have 1 dot left.

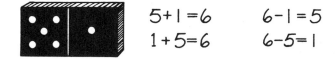

66. Putting On

Objective: Knowledge of addition facts to 18; experience in problem solving

Grade level: 2–3

Group size: Whole class, working in pairs

Materials: Small pictorial and numeral charts (pages 90–91), three regular dice, and game markers

Procedure: This game involving strategy provides practice in addition facts. Students play this game in pairs. The object is to be the player with the lowest score. Each player has a numeral chart and uses the numbers from 1 to 18 on the chart as his or her own playing board. The players take turns rolling the three dice, adding for a total, and covering whatever addends they want that add up to the total roll. For example, if a player rolls 2, 5, and 3, the total is 10, so the player may cover any numbers that add up to 10. One or more markers can be used, but once a numeral is covered, it cannot be used again. Each player continues to cover addends for each roll until he or she cannot cover the total rolled. When both players have reached that point, the game is over. Then both players total their numbers left uncovered. The player with the lowest score is the winner. After one round of play, you could have winners play each other and losers play each other. Have players change partners for each round until only one person has not lost and is the grand winner.

Variation
Use the numbers from 1 to 12 as a playing board. Use only two dice.

67. Adding On with Beans

Objective: Practice in grouping for simple addition and subtraction

Grade level: 1–2

Group size: Whole class or small group

Materials: Small numeral charts (page 91), ten-canisters or multilinks (see page 10), some lima beans, one of the 0 to 9 spinners from the double spinners (pages 109–112), and + and − operational sign circles (page 102)

Procedure: This activity provides students with practice grouping by tens while adding and subtracting beans. You may want to demonstrate the activity on an overhead projector while students do it at their desks. Spin a number and place that many beans, one to a square (starting at 1), on the numeral chart. Spin again and cover that many more spaces. Ask, "How many are covered now?" Spin again and cover more spaces. Ask, "How many spaces are covered now? What always happens when we have ten loose beans?" (we need to make a set of ten) Have students gather the top row of ten loose beans, put them into an empty film canister, and place the canister on the 10 space. Keep adding like this until you reach 100. Make sets of ten when a row is completely covered. Then spin to subtract. Students will have to spill out the last film canister and cover the last row with the loose beans so some can be taken away. Subtract back to 0. This "fill and spill" idea prepares students for regrouping in addition and subtraction. Next you can combine spinning with drawing a sign circle. When students draw a circle with the plus sign, they can add more beans, regrouping if necessary. When they draw a circle with the minus sign, they can take away beans, spilling out more if needed. For first graders, you may want to add only one or two beans at a time, using a bell to indicate when to add the beans. At the end of each row, students should gather the ten loose beans into an empty film canister to make a set of ten. This could be done as a small group activity on the large pictorial or numeral chart. Multilinks are also a good manipulative to use with first graders. When they have ten, they can join the loose multilinks as either a ten-stick or two fives put together and place them on the numeral 10 on the chart.

Variation
Have students record the number sentences on a piece of paper while you use beans on the charts, making sets of ten when necessary. For example, if the first spin is 5, students would record 5 +. And, if the next spin is 3, students

would complete the equation as 5 + 3 = 8. Then they can start the next number sentence with the result of the last one (8). Allow students to practice writing equations and seeing the physical regrouping you do until they reach 100. Then work the same way with subtraction. Begin by placing ten film canisters, each containing ten loose beans, on the pictorial or numeral chart. Have students begin by recording 100 −. Then if you spin 7, for example, spill out a set of ten beans to cover the last ten spaces on the chart. Then take away 7 loose beans to arrive at 93 while students record 100 − 7 = 93. Continue until you arrive back at 0. If some students still need more experience with the manipulatives, work with a small group. Record the sentences as students continue to use the beans and film canisters on the numeral chart.

68. More Fair Trade

Objective: Practice in regrouping in addition and subtraction

Grade level: 3–4

Group size: Small group

Materials: Place value manipulatives (see page 9), place value or tens and ones mats (pages 103–104), pictorial cards made from the large chart (see page 6) or one of the double spinners (pages 109–112), and + and − operational sign circles (page 102)

Procedure: Have each player draw a pictorial card or spin a double spinner and build the amount spun on his or her mat, placing ones on the right side and tens on the left side. Players then take turns drawing a card or spinning a spinner, drawing a sign circle, and adding or subtracting that many beans. This continues for five rounds. Flip a coin to decide if the winner is the player with the most or the least showing on the mat. When adding, encourage students to build the amount spun at the side of the mat before combining it with what is already on the mat and making any necessary trade. When subtracting, encourage them to build the amount spun at the side of the mat, decide with a one-to-one matching technique if that amount can be taken away from what is on the mat, and *then* make any necessary trades before taking away the amount spun. By the third or fourth game, students can usually look at the mat and decide if the amount can be taken away without using the one-to-one matching technique. When you repeat this activity on another day, record the addition and subtraction on a piece of paper in addition to manipulating the place value materials to continue laying the foundation for regrouping in addition and subtraction.

69. Adding and Subtracting with Meaning

Objective: Experience in adding and subtracting two-digit numbers with and without regrouping; understanding the commutative property

Grade level: 2–3

Group size: Whole class or small group

Materials: Addition and subtraction mats (page 105), place value manipulatives (see page 9), acetate or laminated mats, crayons and wipes; and for the variations, pictorial cards made from the large chart (see page 6) and masking tape

Procedure: Have students use a base ten manipulative to build the first addend in the top two boxes. Then have them build the second addend in the middle boxes.

Remind students that adding means to combine, or to pull together. Tell them to combine the ones of both addends and put them in the answer box at the bottom of the mat, trading ten loose ones for a ten and placing it at the top of the tens column if necessary. Encourage them to arrange loose ones in the answer box in a pattern they can recognize without counting. Then tell students to combine all the tens by pulling them down to the answer box at the bottom of the mat. (When it is necessary to form a group of 10 tens and trade them for 1 hundred, extend the grid to three columns of ones, tens, and hundreds.) Ask students to read the answer by looking at the objects in the answer boxes.

While students work the problems with manipulatives, you may want to record the problem using pictures and/or numerals on an overhead projector. Teach problems with and without regrouping at the same time so students will learn to decide if regrouping is necessary each time. When students are confident solving these problems with manipulatives, try having them draw pictures, using sticks and dots for tens and ones. Have students draw a pictorial representation of each two-digit number and then combine them using pictures to show what happens, as well as verbalizing it. Ask students to read their answers and check them with a friend. Spend enough time with the picture stage before adding numerals in the corners of each box. After students have mastered the combined pictures and numerals, have them use just numerals. Be sure to include problems with one two-digit number and one one-digit number, and continue to mix problems with and without regrouping. Also the commutative property of addition can easily be verified by switching the addends positions.

For subtraction, again begin by having students work with manipulatives. Tell students to build the minuend in the first two boxes and to write numerals for the subtrahend in the middle two boxes. Then they will have to make a decision as to whether the ones amount in the subtrahend can be taken away from the minuend ones amount. If so, have students take away that many of the objects from the minuend and place them in the ones box of the second row. Then tell them to move the objects that are left to the answer box at the bottom of the page. If the ones amount cannot be taken away, students will have to break a ten-stick into ones. After students have completed renaming, remind them to check to see that the total amount is still the same. Explain to students that numbers can have more than one name. After students have subtracted the ones, have them subtract the tens. Be sure to mix problems with and without regrouping to encourage students to evaluate the problem. Students should also verbalize what has happened. While students work the problems with manipulatives, you may want to do them on an overhead projector and begin to combine drawing pictures and using symbols while you talk about what is happening. When students are ready to draw pictures for subtraction, have them first draw the total amount and write the numerals for what is to be taken away. Then they will have to decide if renaming is necessary. If so, have them draw a picture of the renamed number by moving over one ten stick and showing it as ten ones. Finally, have them write in numerals what is left in the answer boxes at the bottom of the mat. When students have mastered the combined pictures and numerals, have them use just numerals.

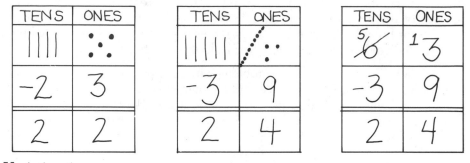

Variation 1

Have students choose two large pictorial cards and place them on the mat so the mat's center line divides the tens and ones on each card. For addition, instruct them to look at the pictures and write the answer in numerals in the bottom boxes. The commutative property of addition can easily be verified by switching the cards positions.

For subtraction, have students place the greater number on the top boxes. Ask students to compare the two numbers, find the difference, and see how many more in the top number than in the other number. To find out how much more, they can compare the pictures with a one-to-one matching. Tell them to look at the ones on the second card and decide if there are enough ones on the top card for a one-to-one matching. If not, some more ones will be needed. Students can move the top card just slightly to the right so a ten stick is now with the ones. Ask students to decide how many more ones are on the top card now and to write the answer as a numeral. Finally, have them compare the tens and write the answer as a numeral.

Variation 2

Use masking tape to make a large grid like the one on the addition and subtraction mat on the floor. Then do this activity using students as the manipulative. To make a ten, ten students can stand close together and hold hands.

70. Mental Addition

Objective:	Practice adding and comparing visually
Grade level:	2–3 (Variations 2 and 3: 3–4)
Group size:	Whole class, playing in pairs
Materials:	Pictorial cards made from the small chart (see page 7)
Procedure:	After you have taught addition with and without regrouping using manipulatives, use this pictorial activity. Have two students work together. Each one draws a pair of pictorial cards, adds them visually, and has the other student verify the answer. Then they place each pair of cards in one of two piles: no regrouping problems and regrouping problems. Encourage discussion. This would also be a good time to talk about the commutative property of addition.

Variation 1

Try having students draw two pictorial cards and compare them visually to find the difference (subtract the smaller from the larger). Again sort into no regrouping and regrouping piles.

Variation 2

Have students try to add three or four pictorial cards at once. They can check each other's answers on a calculator. Notice how easy it is to make sets of ten from the "5 plus some more" arrangement of the ones and tens.

Variation 3

In this game, one player draws two or three cards, estimates the sum to the nearest ten, and writes the answer. The other player uses a calculator to check the addition and determine if the estimate is reasonable. Players trade roles and keep track of how well each one estimated. If necessary, have a small pictorial or numeral chart available to check the rounding (see Activity 63).

71. Arrow Games

Objective:	Experience in directional adding and subtracting
Grade level:	2–4
Group size:	Whole class
Materials:	Small numeral charts (page 91), acetate sheets, and crayons and wipes; and for the variation, a giant 1 to 100 chart (see page 10)
Procedure:	Introduce arrow math silently, writing the following numbers and arrows on the chalkboard without saying a word. (Or, write them on an overhead projector or large cards that you can hold up in front of the class. You can also put them on small cards for work with individual students at a learning center.)

$$5 \rightarrow 6$$
$$5 \downarrow \downarrow 25$$
$$4 \downarrow 14$$
$$47 \uparrow 37$$
$$12 \leftarrow \underline{?}$$
$$23 \rightarrow \rightarrow \underline{?}$$

When you write a blank with a question mark, offer the piece of chalk to the class, beckoning someone to fill in the number. Using only actions, not words, help the class understand that each arrow shows what direction to move on the numeral chart.

$\longrightarrow$ +1	$\longleftarrow$ −1	$\downarrow$ +10	$\uparrow$ −10

- As you continue to present arrow math problems, the students should use either the large numeral chart and a pointer or small charts at their desks to find the starting number, follow the arrows, and then name the ending number. Here are some examples, with answers in parentheses.

  1. 12 → → (14)
  2. 47 ← ← (45)
  3. 15 → ↑ (6)
  4. 62 ← → (62)
  5. 18 ↓ ↓ (38)
  6. 49 ↑ ← (38)
  7. 92 → ↑ ↑ (73)
  8. 5 ↓ ↓ → (26)
  9. 79 ↑ ↑ ↑ (49)
  10. 18 ← ↓ → (28)
  11. 56 ← ← ← (53)
  12. 84 → ↑ → (76)
  13. 6 → ↓ → ↓ (28)
  14. 54 ↑ ← ↑ ← (32)
  15. 11 ↓ ↓ → → ↑ ↓ (33)
  16. 24 ↓ ↓ → → → ↑ (37)
  17. 35 ↑ ↑ ← ← ↑ ← (2)
  18. 73 ↓ ↓ ↓ → → ↑ → (96)

Did your students discover short cuts? (Arrows sometimes cancel each other out.)

- Ask students to write the rule and then the equation for arrow math problems, as in the following examples.

  12 → →   RULE: +2   EQUATION: 12 + 1 + 1 = 14
  54 ↑ ← ↑ ←   RULE: −22   EQUATION: 54 − 10 − 1 − 10 − 1 = 32

- Write the following arrow paths on the chalkboard. Ask students to give the rule for each one.

  → ↓ (+11)   ← ↑ (−11)   → ↑ ↑ (−19)
  ↓ ← ← ← (+7)   ↓ → → ↑ ← (+1)

- Write the following arrows and ending numbers on the chalkboard. Ask students to give the starting number for each one.
  1. _?_ ↓ → ↓ → 55   (Starting number: 33)
  2. _?_ ← ← ↑ ↓ 87   (Starting number: 89)
  3. _?_ ↓ ↓ → 49   (Starting number: 28)
  4. _?_ ↓ ↑ → ← ↓ 14   (Starting number: 4)

5. _?_ ↑ ↑ → → → 20   *(Starting number: 37)*
6. _?_ ↓ ← ↓ → ↓ 100   *(Starting number: 70)*
7. _?_ ↓ ↑ → → ← ← 75   *(Starting number: 55)*
8. _?_ ↓ ↓ ↓ ← ← 61   *(Starting number: 33)*
9. _?_ ↑ ← ↓ → ↑ ↓ 32   *(Starting number: 32)*

- Ask students to draw an arrow path to get from the first number to the second number for each of the following pairs. The order of arrows in the answers may vary.

1. 7 to 16 (← ↓)
2. 67 to 54 (← ← ← ↑)
3. 34 to 66 (→ → ↓ ↓ ↓)
4. 25 to 43 (← ← ↓ ↓)
5. 45 to 28 (↑ ↑ → → →)
6. 86 to 53 (↑ ↑ ↑ ← ← ←)

Variation (Active)
Do this activity on a giant 1 to 100 chart in the gym.

72. More Arrow Games

Objective: Practice with directionality on a 1 to 100 chart

Grade level: 3–4

Group size: Whole class

Materials: Small numeral charts (page 91), acetate sheets, and crayons and wipes; and for the variation, a giant 1 to 100 chart (see page 10)

Procedure: Add diagonal arrows to the horizontal and vertical arrows introduced in Activity 71.

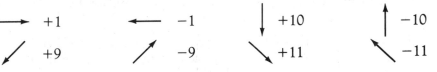

→ +1   ← −1   ↓ +10   ↑ −10
↙ +9   ↗ −9   ↘ +11   ↖ −11

Students should find the starting number, follow the arrows, and name the ending number. Ask them to state the rule and write the equation.

1. 37 ↘ ↖

   (15; RULE: −22; EQUATION: 37 − 11 − 11 = 15)

2. 54 ← ↗

   (62; RULE: +8; EQUATION: 54 − 1 + 9 = 62)

3. 4 ↘ ↑

   (5; RULE: +1; EQUATION: 4 + 11 − 10 = 5)

4. 72 ↓ ↘

   (93; RULE: +21; EQUATION: 72 + 10 + 11 = 93)

5. 61 ↗ ←

(51; RULE: −10; EQUATION: 61 − 9 − 1 = 51)

6. 60 ← ↘ ↑

(38; RULE: −22; EQUATION: 60 − 1 − 10 − 11 = 38)

7. 29 ↓ ↘ ↑

(40; RULE: +11; EQUATION: 29 + 10 + 11 − 10 = 40)

8. 14 ↘ ↓ ↙

(44; RULE: +30; EQUATION: 14 + 11 + 10 + 9 = 44)

9. 34 ↘ ↑ → ↘

(47; RULE: +13; EQUATION: 34 + 11 − 10 + 1 + 11 = 47)

10. 25 ↗ ↓ → ↙

(36; RULE: +11; EQUATION: 25 − 9 + 10 + 1 + 9 = 36)

11. 86 ← ↑ → ↘ ↓

(97; RULE: +11; EQUATION: 86 − 1 − 10 + 1 + 11 + 10 = 97)

12. 100 ↘ ↘ ← ↑ → ↓ ↗

(69; RULE: −31; EQUATION: 100 − 11 − 11 − 1 − 10 + 1 + 10 − 9 = 69)

Variation (Active)
Do this activity on a giant 1 to 100 chart in the gym.

73. Race to Find the Answer

Objective: Practice in adding and subtracting mentally through visual imagery; practice listening

Grade level: 3–4

Group size: Whole class

Materials: Small numeral charts (page 91) and game markers; and for the variation, a giant 1 to 100 chart (see page 10)

Procedure: Following arrow math, students begin to see how easy it is to add and subtract on the numeral chart. Dictate a problem to the class; for example: "Start at 16, (*pause*), add 20." Students should point to 16, move down two columns, and cover the answer, 36, with a marker. Start with some easy problems:

1. Start at 54, minus 20 (*up two*—34)
2. Start at 22, plus 30 (*down three*—52)
3. Start at 77, minus 10 (*up one*—67)
4. Start at 6, plus 40 (*down four*—46)
5. Start at 62, plus 4 (*right four*—66)
6. Start at 87, minus 6 (*left six*—81)
7. Start at 58, plus 5 (*right five*—63)
8. Start at 12, minus 3 (*left three*—9)

Continue with problems that are a bit harder. (Dictate slowly, pause between numbers.)

9. Start at 16, plus 21 (*down two, right one*—37; *or right one, down two*—37)
10. Start at 93, minus 32 (*up three, left two*—61; *or left two, up three*—61)

11. Start at 50, plus 27 (*down two, right seven—77; or right seven, down two—77*)
12. Start at 76, minus 41 (*up four, left one—35; or left one, up four—35*)
13. Start at 82, minus 17 (*up one, left seven—65; or left seven, up one—65*)

Then finish with the hardest problems. (Dictate slowly, pause between numbers.)

14. Start at 16,	+21	+15		(*52*)
15. Start at 49,	−24	− 6		(*19*)
16. Start at 62,	+10	+21		(*93*)
17. Start at 29,	+32	−24		(*37*)
18. Start at 9,	+21	− 4	+32	(*58*)
19. Start at 75,	−33	− 2	+28	(*68*)
20. Start at 43,	+17	+ 5	−24	(*41*)
21. Start at 52,	−10	+14	+36	(*92*)

After you have used the numeral chart for adding and subtracting with arrow math, see if students can do some simple problems with their eyes closed. Give them problems without regrouping first.

Variation (Active)
Do this activity on a giant 1 to 100 chart in the gym.

74. Race to 100 and Back

Objective:	Practice in mental addition
Grade level:	3–4
Group size:	Whole class, playing in pairs
Materials:	Small numeral charts (page 91), one of the double spinners (pages 109–112), game markers; and for the variation, a giant 1 to 100 chart (see page 10)
Procedure:	To start, the two players each place a marker next to 1. The first player spins the spinner and moves that number of spaces on his or her chart. Then the next player spins and moves his or her marker the correct number of spaces. Players alternate taking turns. When players reach 100, they go backwards. The first player to arrive back at 1 is the winner. This is a very quick-moving game.

Variation (Active)
Play on the giant 1 to 100 chart in the gym.

75. Odd/Even Sums

Objective:	Practice in adding to 100; experience in problem solving
Grade level:	3–4
Group size:	Whole class
Materials:	Sets of numeral cards made from the small chart (see page 7) and three cards labeled as shown below.

Procedure: Each student draws twenty pairs of numeral cards. The pairs of cards are sorted into three piles: even and odd; even and even; and odd and odd. Have students add each pair of numbers and try to draw some conclusions about the sums of the different kinds of pairs. Have manipulatives available to help students verify their conclusions.

Variation
Have each student mix a set of numeral cards and place the cards on the desk facedown. Then tell them to draw two cards and add the numbers. If the sum is even, students should set the pair aside; if not, they should place the cards back into the pool. Have students keep drawing two cards and following this procedure. Ask, "What happens if you play long enough?" (Every card will be matched.)

76. Signs in a Sentence

Objective: Understanding of number sentences; experience in problem solving

Grade level: 3–4

Group size: Whole class

Materials: Pictorial and numeral cards made from the small charts (see page 7) and sign circles (page 102); and for the variation, pictorial and numeral cards made from the large charts (see page 6) and large sign circles (page 101)

Procedure: Review the four relational symbols: $=$, $\neq$, $>$, $<$. Discuss how these symbols are used to show how things are related to one another. Talk about the meaning of each. Remind students that *every* mathematical sentence needs a relational symbol to convey a complete mathematical idea. Point out that the plus and minus operational symbols show what to do with the things in the sentence and are used only if appropriate to make a true mathematical sentence. Using the picture or numeral cards, have students make as many true number sentences as they can in five minutes. When you say, "Stop," each student records the number sentences on paper. Encourage students to have friends check their number sentences. You can collect the papers to check the students' work.

Variation
Use the large sign circles with the large pictorial and numeral cards for learning center activities. You will need plus and minus operational symbols to add to the relational signs from page 101. Ask each student to arrange and record as many true sentences as he or she can in a given time. Then try it again!

77. What's the Sum?

Objective: Experience in problem solving

Grade level: 3–4

Group size: Whole class

Materials: Small numeral charts (page 91) and paper and pencils

Procedure: Adding consecutive numbers on the numeral chart reveals many interesting patterns. Let students use a calculator for adding in this activity. Have them add consecutive numbers in pairs, sets of three, sets of four, and so on. Have students try to find the pattern in each set. You may want to write the following charts on the chalkboard. Ask, "Do you notice any relationships from one group to the next? Can you draw any conclusions?" (Notice that in each set the difference between consecutive sums is the square of the number of numbers being added.)

2 NUMBERS	SUM	3 NUMBERS	SUM	4 NUMBERS	SUM
1 + 2	3)4	1 + 2 + 3	6)9	1 + 2 + 3 + 4	10)16
3 + 4	7)4	4 + 5 + 6	15)9	5 + 6 + 7 + 8	26)16
5 + 6	11)4	7 + 8 + 9	24)9	9 + 10 + 11 + 12	42)16
7 + 8	15)4	10 + 11 + 12	33)9	13 + 14 + 15 + 16	58)16
9 + 10	19)4	13 + 14 + 15	42)9	17 + 18 + 19 + 20	74)16
11 + 12	23	16 + 17 + 18	51	21 + 22 + 23 + 24	90

Variation

For another problem-solving question, ask, "What is the sum of the numbers from 1 to 100?" Help students by having them first think about a simpler case, such as the sum of numbers from 1 to 10. In this case, have them pair the numbers as shown below.

1 2 3 4 5 6 7 8 9 10   SUM: 55

Then ask, "Could you pair the numbers from 1 to 100?" Encourage students to think about and explain their thinking strategies.

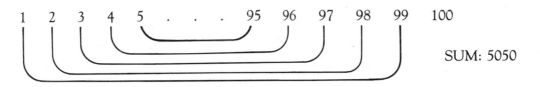

1 2 3 4 5 . . . 95 96 97 98 99 100   SUM: 5050

78. Place Them Right

Objective: Experience in problem solving

Grade level: 3–4

Group size: Whole class

Materials: Numeral cards made from the small chart (see page 7), and paper and pencil

Procedure: On a piece of paper, have students draw _____ + _____ = _____ six times in a column. Then have them sort out the cards from 1 to 20. Have students place 18 of these numeral cards on the lines to make six true sentences. They will have to keep moving the numbers around until they find a solution. Tell them to record their solutions. Ask, "Can you find another solution?" Have students draw _____◯_____ = _____ four times in a column. Then using *all* the numeral cards, have students draw 12 cards at random. Ask them to see if they can use the 12 cards to make four true sentences. The sentences can be addition sentences, subtraction sentences, or a mixture. Students can write the appropriate signs for their sentences in the small circles. Again, they will have to keep moving the cards around until they find a solution.

Encourage them not to give up too quickly. Tell them to record their solutions and to try again with 12 different cards.

79. Inners and Outers

Objective: Experience in problem solving and patterns

Grade level: 3–4

Group size: Whole class

Materials: Small pictorial or numeral charts (pages 90–91), paper and pencils, and calculators

Procedure: Let students use a calculator for adding in this activity. Ask students to choose any four numbers in a row, column, or diagonal on the numeral chart. Tell them to find the sum of the outer two numbers and then the sum of the inner two numbers. Ask, "What do you notice about the sums in each case?" (They are the same.) "Can you explain why this works?" (In a row, moving right increases one addend by one, and moving left decreases the other addend by one, so the sum stays the same: In a column, the addends are ten more and ten less, and in a diagonal the addends are eleven [or nine] more and less.)

EXAMPLES:

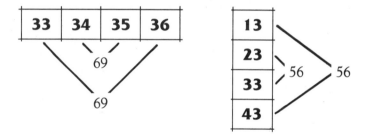

Variation
Try this activity with numbers that are two squares apart or three squares apart on the numeral chart.

EXAMPLES:

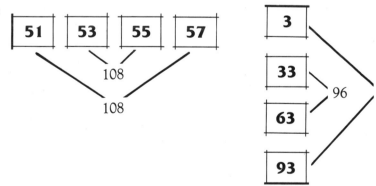

80. Expanding Cross

Objective: Experience in problem solving and patterns

Grade level: 3–4

Group size: Whole class

Materials: Small pictorial or numeral charts (pages 90–91), paper and pencils, and calculators

64

Procedure: Let students use a calculator for adding in this activity. Ask students to choose any number and add it four times. Then tell them to add the four numbers that surround the original number on the numeral chart. They should keep going out on the arms of the cross and adding each set of four numbers. Ask, "What is true about the sums?" (They are the same.) "Why?" (The four numbers that surround the original number include numbers that are one more, one less, ten more, and ten less than the original number. The one more and one less numbers balance as do the ten more and ten less numbers, so the sum of the four numbers equals the sum of four of the original numbers. The same principle works for the next four numbers, which are two and twenty more and less than the original number.)

EXAMPLE:

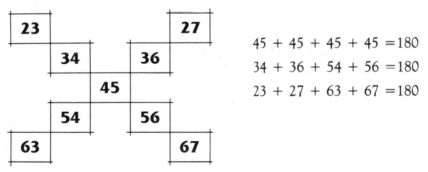

$$33 + 33 + 33 + 33 = 132$$
$$23 + 32 + 34 + 43 = 132$$
$$13 + 31 + 35 + 53 = 132$$

Variation

Try this activity with numbers in an X formation on the numeral chart. Ask, "Does it still work?" (Yes.) "Why?" (The principle discussed in the main activity applies here. On one diagonal, the numbers are nine more and less; on the other diagonal they are eleven more and less.)

EXAMPLE:

23				27
	34		36	
		45		
	54		56	
63				67

$$45 + 45 + 45 + 45 = 180$$
$$34 + 36 + 54 + 56 = 180$$
$$23 + 27 + 63 + 67 = 180$$

81. Adding Squares

Objective: Experience in problem solving and patterns

Grade level: 3–4

Group size: Whole class

Materials: Small pictorial or numeral charts (pages 90–91), paper and pencils, and calculators

Procedure: Let students use a calculator for adding in this activity. Ask students to put a square around any 2 × 2, 3 × 3, or 4 × 4 square of numbers on the chart and then add the numbers in the diagonals. Ask, "What do you notice?" (The sums are the same.) Encourage them to try adding only opposite corners on the diagonals and to try some rectangles or parallelograms. Ask, "What do you notice?" (The sums are the same.) "Will it always work?" (Yes, the order of the 1 to 100 chart, with the patterns discussed in Activities 79 and 80, ensures this will always work.)

EXAMPLES:

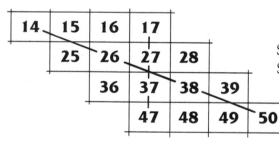

21	22
31	32

SUM OF DIAGONALS: 53

53	54	55
63	64	65
73	74	75

SUM OF DIAGONALS: 192

27	28	29	30
37	38	39	40
47	48	49	50
57	58	59	60

SUM OF DIAGONALS: 174
SUM OF OPPOSITE CORNERS: 87

SUM OF DIAGONALS: 128
SUM OF OPPOSITE CORNERS: 64

6

Multiplication and Division Activities

Multiplication and addition are closely linked, and students' understanding of them should develop simultaneously. Multiplication is a repeated combining of sets, or repeated addition. Similarly, division is closely linked to subtraction. Division is apportioning a whole into equal parts, or repeated subtraction. Addition and multiplication are putting sets together to get a total, while subtraction and division are just the reverse—taking apart, or apportioning, the total. In Part 6 the 1 to 100 charts are used as a tool to help teach multiplication and division.

82. Building Arrays

Objective: Understanding the concept of multiplication and the commutative property

Grade level: 2–3

Group size: Whole class

Materials: Small blank charts (page 92), some game markers in one color; and for the variations, a giant blank chart (see page 10) or acetate and crayons and wipes

Procedure: Building an orderly arrangement (an array) is one of the easiest ways to teach the concepts of multiplication and the commutative property at the same time. Students use the blank chart as an organizer for the sets of markers. Have students build a set of three markers somewhere on the chart. Have them build another set of three markers just below the first set and then a third set and a fourth set. Say, "You have built four sets of three chips each." Ask students the following kinds of questions: "How many sets have you built? How many markers are in each set? How many markers are there in all? Can you count by threes?" Say, "Four different times you made a group of three. We say four times three equals twelve." Then, without moving the array, rotate the paper 90° so that students see three sets of four chips each. Say, "Three different times you see a set of four markers. We say three times four equals twelve." Discuss the commutative property of multiplication and look at arrays from both directions. Decide at what point to show students how to write the sentence in abstract form. Students could build some of their own arrays and discuss them with a friend. For students to understand multiplication as the concept of repeated sets, build and rotate other arrays and ask the same questions.

Variation 1
Use the small blank grid under acetate and have students draw pictures instead of using markers. Have students record both number sentences along the sides of the picture.

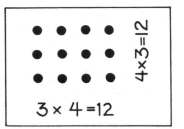

Variation 2 (Active)
Do this activity on the giant blank chart using children's bodies or large objects.

83. Guess My Rule Multiplication

Objective:	Discovering counting patterns for multiplication
Grade level:	2–3
Group size:	Whole class
Materials:	Small numeral charts (page 91), game markers, and paper and pencil
Procedure:	Use the "guess my rule" format for discovering the patterns in the multiplication tables. Draw pictures and/or use numerals to fill in the "guess my rule" charts. Then, cover the numerals on the 1 to 100 chart to see the patterns emerge.

TRIANGLES	SIDES
△	3
△ △	6
△ △ △	9
△ △ △ △	12

Ideas for developing multiplication

by 1's	unicycles/wheels	unicorns/horns
by 2's	people/eyes	bicycles/wheels
by 3's	triangles/sides	tricycles/wheels
by 4's	squares/sides	home runs/bases touched
by 5's	stars/points	hands/fingers, nickels/pennies
by 6's	hexagons/sides	six packs/bottles
by 7's	weeks/days	
by 8's	octagons/sides	octopuses/arms

84. Multiplication Patterns

Objective: Recognition of patterns in multiplication

Grade level: 3–4

Group size: Whole class

Materials: Small numeral charts (page 91) and some game markers in one color

Procedure: Introduce multiplication on the numeral chart using patterns to help build visual imagery and understanding. This activity could take several weeks or a month to complete. Do one pattern a day and use a different color for each pattern. Follow the steps given below for each multiplication table.

1. Cover the numerals for each set of multiples with one color of markers. For example, for the multiples of 3 cover with a marker every third number from 1 to 100.

1	2	(3)	4	5	(6)	7	8	(9)	10
11	(12)	13	14	(15)	16	17	(18)	19	20
(21)	22	23	(24)	25	26	(27)	28	29	(30)

2. Discuss the pattern thoroughly. Students will see different things. Look across rows and down columns. (See step 6.)
3. Practice counting the numerals covered on the chart: 3, 6, 9, 12, 15 .... Count backwards too: 30, 27, 24, 21, 18 .... Ask, "What is four 3's? two 3's? seven 3's?" List the numbers on the chalkboard as they are called.
4. Have students put colored dots in the squares to record each pattern on their numeral charts, using a different chart and color for each times table. Display several of these tables around the room.
5. Point out how the pattern in the ending digits keeps repeating on the chart. Have students count aloud the pattern of ending digits. Make the pattern of ending digits obvious by writing the following lists on the chalkboard. Write the ones digits in colored chalk. Note how each pair of tables shows two patterns whose ending digits are the reverse of each other.

	1's			9's	
1	11	21	9	99	189
2	12	22	18	108	198
3	13	23	27	117	207
4	14	24	36	126	216
5	15	25	45	135	225
6	16	26	54	144	234
7	17	27	63	153	243
8	18	28	72	162	252
9	19	29	81	171	261
10	20	30	90	180	270

	2's				8's	
2	12	22		8	48	88
4	14	24		16	56	96
6	16	26		24	64	104
8	18	28		32	72	112
10	20	30		40	80	120

	3's				7's	
3	33	63		7	77	147
6	36	66		14	84	153
9	39	69		21	91	161
12	42	72		28	98	168
15	45	75		35	105	175
18	48	78		42	112	182
21	51	81		49	119	189
24	54	84		56	126	196
27	57	87		63	133	203
30	60	90		70	140	210

	4's				6's	
4	24	44		6	36	66
8	28	48		12	42	72
12	32	52		18	48	78
16	36	56		24	54	84
20	40	60		30	60	90

			5's		
5	15	25	35	45	55
10	20	30	40	50	60

6. Have students make booklets where they can order and compare all the patterns. Encourage them to continue looking for patterns and relationships among the charts.

Cover with chips	Pattern
every numeral	plus one
every 2nd numeral	five columns covered (odd/even)
every 3rd numeral	diagonals slanted to right
every 4th numeral	compare to 2's pattern
every 5th numeral	two columns covered
every 6th numeral	compare to 2's and 4's patterns
every 7th numeral	look at diagonals and columns
every 8th numeral	compare to 2's, 4's, and 6's patterns
every 9th numeral	diagonals slanted to right; compare to 3's pattern
every 10th numeral	one column, compare to 2's and 5's patterns
every 11th numeral	diagonal slanted to left
every 12th numeral	compare columns to 2's, 4's, 6's, and 8's patterns

Variation 1

For further experience with the ending digits pattern of the multiplication tables, have students draw the house shown below so that it almost fills a sheet of paper. Be sure they include the dots and numerals. Then have them draw lines to connect the dots in different ways, following the pattern of ending digits for each set of multiples. Students use a different color for each pattern as listed below.

- Multiples of 2—red
  (2, 4, 6, 8, 0, 2 ...)
- Multiples of 8—brown
  (8, 6, 4, 2, 0, 8 ...)
- Multiples of 3—green
  (3, 6, 9, 2, 5, 8, 1, 4, 7, 0, 3 ...)
- Multiples of 7—black
  (7, 4, 1, 8, 5, 2, 9, 6, 3, 0, 7 ...)
- Multiples of 4—purple
  (4, 8, 2, 6, 0, 4 ...)
- Multiples of 6—blue
  (6, 2, 8, 4, 0, 6 ...)
- Multiples of 5—yellow
  (5, 0, 5 ...)

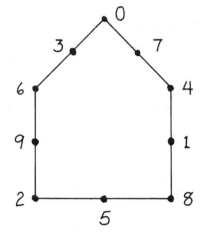

Variation 2

Another way to introduce multiplication patterns is by using students' names. Give each student a small numeral chart. Tell students to write their first name repeatedly from left to right in a continuous line, using one box for each letter. Letters can be printed to the right of the numerals. Have students choose a different color for each letter in their names. Then have them color the name pattern until the numeral chart is completely covered. After all students have colored their name charts, ask all the three-letter names to count aloud using the last letter of their name. (3, 6, 9, 12, 15, 18 ...) Then try using the first letter of their name. (1, 4, 7, 10, 13, 16 ...) And, finally, the middle letter of their name. (2, 5, 8, 11, 14, 17 ...) Point out that it's always counting by threes, no matter where you begin. Try this same thing with the four-letter names, the five-letter names, and so on until every student has counted by the number of letters in his or her name. Encourage students to find others in the room with the same pattern and compare their charts.

85. Counting On

Objective: Practice counting by twos, threes, fours, and fives, starting at any number

Grade level: 3

Group size: Whole class

Materials: Small numeral charts (page 91), one of the double spinners (pages 109–112), game markers, Popsicle sticks marked with 2, 3, 4 or 5 dots; and for Variation 3, a giant 1 to 100 chart

Procedure: This activity gives students experience with sequenced number patterns. Mix up the Popsicle sticks and place them in a box. Spin the spinner and call out the number. Instruct students to place a marker on that number. Then draw a Popsicle stick and say, for example, "Count on by threes." Starting with the number already covered, the students place markers on the chart to count in that sequence. Write the beginning number on the chalkboard and have students call out the number that comes next in the sequence. Continue with that pattern for two or three rows.

Variation 1
Play in the same way, but count backwards from the spun number in the sequence indicated on the Popsicle stick. Record the number sequence.

Variation 2
Spin a number and use it as the middle of the sequence. Count both forwards and backwards as indicated on the Popsicle stick. Show how to record the number sequence.

Variation 3 (Active)
Use the giant numeral chart in the gym or hall to do this activity by having students walk the number sequences.

86. Complete the Pattern

Objective: Recognition of number patterns
Grade level: 3–4
Group size: Whole class
Materials: Small numeral charts (page 91), game markers, and copies of the Complete the Patterns worksheet on page 127
Procedure: Tell students to study the number patterns and to fill in the blanks. The markers can be used to cover the known numbers in each pattern on the chart. This helps students discover the missing parts. After the worksheet is completed, discuss each number pattern.

87. Multiplication Drill with Dominoes

Objective: Knowledge of multiplication facts, commutative property, and mathematical sentences
Grade level: 3–4
Group size: Individuals
Materials: Set of double nine dominoes, small numeral chart (page 91) for reference, and paper and pencil
Procedure: Review the commutative property of multiplication with individual students at a learning center. Using a double nine set of dominoes, have the student draw a domino out of a bag and write the two multiplication sentences for the two numbers on the domino. If needed, the student can use the small numeral chart for reference (or the multiplication patterns booklet made in Activity 84).

$$7 \times 4 = 28$$
$$4 \times 7 = 28$$

88. Division Fun

Objective: Understanding the concept of division and remainders

Grade level: 3–4

Group size: Small group

Materials: Loose beans, small paper cups; and for the variation, small numeral charts (page 91), one of the double spinners (pages 109–112), game markers, regular die, acetate, and crayons and wipes

Procedure: This activity works best in a small group where you can watch each child carefully. When teaching division as a sharing concept, begin with something concrete like a bag of pennies or a handful of beans. Have each student get some small cups, take a handful of beans, estimate how many they have, then divide or share their set into equivalent subsets with a given size. After students use the cups to make all the equivalent subsets possible, the leftovers, the remainder, go on the table. Tell the students to count their beans by the amount in each cup and add the remainder to get the total for their handful of beans. Ask, "How many beans in each cup (subset size)? How many cups (subsets) are there? How many beans in all? If you poured out all the beans on the table, how many would there be?" Try several such division problems. Next, repeat the activity, having students use the same handful of beans and the number of cups you specify.

Variation

Provide each student with a small numeral chart and some markers to indicate each subset. Spin one of the double spinners for the set total that is to be divided; then throw a die to determine the number in each subset. Use the markers to count subsets. For example, if 4 was the number on the die, students would cover every fourth number with one marker until the number on the spinner is reached. Ask, "Did you have a remainder, some extra squares less than a subset of four?" Count the number of markers laid down to determine the number of subsets. Then count the extra squares as the remainder. (They could also begin at the number and go backwards, repeatedly subtracting 4 until there is less than a subset of four as the remainder.) You can also have students do this activity with the numeral chart under acetate by marking X's for each subset. Show students how this kind of problem is written. If students have made colored dots to show the multiplication patterns on their numeral charts in Activity 84, they could use them to figure out each answer. For example, to determine how many fours are in 41, show students how to look at the colored pattern chart for fours, find 41, count the subsets, and then count the remaining squares that do not form another complete subset. For 41 there are ten sets of four squares and one remaining square, or $41 \div 4 = 10\,R1$. Challenge students to see who can find the answer the quickest.

1	2	3	4	5	6	7	8	9	10
11	12	13	14	15	16	17	18	19	20
21	22	23	24	25	26	27	28	29	30
31	32	33	34	35	36	37	38	39	40
(41)	42	43	44	45	46	47	48	49	50

89. Factors and Multiples

Objective: Experience in multiplication, ; discovering the prime numbers

Grade level: 4

Group size: Whole class

Materials: Small numeral charts (page 91), game markers of several colors, or multilinks and crayons

Procedure: Each child covers all the multiples of 2 with red chips, all the multiples of 3 with green chips, all the multiples of 4 with purple chips, and all the multiples of 5 with yellow chips. (Or, use different colors of crayons or multilinks.) Discuss the language used in multiplication: 12 is a *multiple* of 2, 3, and 4; 2, 3, and 4 are *factors* of 12; and 12 is the *product* of the factors 3 and 4. When students are ready, also practice multiples of 6 and greater. Point out that some of the numbers are not covered, and introduce the concepts of primes and composites (see Extension).

Extension

In this activity for discovering the primes, each student begins with a copy of the numeral hundreds chart and a pencil. Discuss how the number 1 is unique: it is a factor of every number; it is the identity element for multiplication; it is neither prime nor composite. Have students draw a box around 1. Explain that when a whole number greater than 1 has only 1 and itself as factors, it is called a *prime number.* Instruct students to circle the primes and cross out all the multiples on their charts. Help them start by circling 2 and crossing out the other multiples of 2: 4, 6, 8, 10 . . . 100. Since the only factors of 3 are 1 and 3, students should circle 3 and cross out all remaining multiples of 3: 9, 15, 21 . . . 99. (Continuing, 4 has been crossed out, so the next numeral not circled or crossed out is 5. Students should circle 5 and cross out the remaining multiples of 5: 25, 35, 55, . . . 100. Point out that many of the multiples of 5 have already been crossed out because some are also multiples of 2 or 3. The next numeral not crossed out is 7. Students should circle 7 and cross out the remaining multiples of 7: 63, 77, 91 . . . 98. The next numeral not crossed out is 11, so students circle 11. At this point, students will observe that all the multiples of 11 (other than 11 itself) have been crossed out. Ask, "What generalization can you make about the multiples of 13?" (All multiples of 13, other than 13 itself, have already been crossed out.)

[1]	(2)	(3)	~~4~~	(5)	~~6~~	(7)	~~8~~	~~9~~	~~10~~
(11)	~~12~~	(13)	~~14~~	~~15~~	~~16~~	(17)	~~18~~	(19)	~~20~~
~~21~~	~~22~~	(23)	~~24~~	~~25~~	~~26~~	~~27~~	~~28~~	(29)	~~30~~
(31)	~~32~~	~~33~~	~~34~~	~~35~~	~~36~~	(37)	~~38~~	~~39~~	~~40~~
(41)	~~42~~	(43)	~~44~~	~~45~~	~~46~~	(47)	~~48~~	~~49~~	~~50~~
~~51~~	~~52~~	(53)	~~54~~	~~55~~	~~56~~	~~57~~	~~58~~	(59)	~~60~~
(61)	~~62~~	~~63~~	~~64~~	~~65~~	~~66~~	(67)	~~68~~	~~69~~	~~70~~
(71)	~~72~~	(73)	~~74~~	~~75~~	~~76~~	~~77~~	~~78~~	(79)	~~80~~
~~81~~	~~82~~	(83)	~~84~~	~~85~~	~~86~~	~~87~~	~~88~~	(89)	~~90~~
~~91~~	~~92~~	~~93~~	~~94~~	~~95~~	~~96~~	(97)	~~98~~	~~99~~	~~100~~

Have students verify this generalization using a calculator. Ask, "Can you further generalize about the numerals that have not been crossed out? Did you notice that all the prime numbers except 2 are odd? Why is this true?" (Every even number has 2 as a factor.) Explain that a whole number greater than 1 that has only 1 and itself as factors is called a *prime number,* and a whole number greater than 1 that has whole number factors other than 1 and itself is called a *composite number.*

Money
Activities

Before introducing the money activities in this section, examine our coins and discuss them with your students, talking about their size and thickness, their edges, and their metal composition. Observe and discuss both sides of each coin, look at the inscriptions, and make rubbings. Do a lot of sorting as students learn to discriminate among the coin attributes. Be sure to use the names of the coins as you talk about them so students will begin to associate the names with the coins. Use real coins during the early stages of discovery.

In the activities that follow, the 1 to 100 chart corresponds to a dollar bill, and is used to teach the values of the coins, how to count and compare coin amounts, and how to make change to a dollar. Play money and the money cut-outs are also used in the activities. This is a good time to begin to develop students' insight into fractional parts. The 1 to 100 chart can be seen as a whole, and then a coin's value can be seen as a part of that whole.

90. Place Value Review

Objective: Learning the value and name of the penny and dime

Grade level: 1–2

Group size: Whole class

Materials: Small pictorial or numeral charts (pages 90–91), penny and dime cut-outs (page 117), some play dimes and pennies; and for the variation, small blank charts (page 92)

Procedure: Have students use either the pictorial or numeral chart to discover how many spaces a penny cut-out covers on the 1 to 100 chart. Say, "A penny is worth

one cent." Then have them find out how many spaces a dime strip covers. Say "A dime is worth ten cents." Ask them how many penny cut-outs it takes to cover the whole chart and how many dime strips it takes to cover it. Ask how many penny cut-outs and dime strips it takes to cover 60¢, 40¢, 80¢, 24¢, 56¢, and so on. Then use play money in the same way. Students can place a penny on a single space and a dime at the end of ten spaces. Tell students to place six dimes on the chart and count the total: "ten, twenty, thirty, forty, fifty, sixty cents." Then have students place down different amounts of pennies and dimes that you give them and count the amounts. Encourage them to put down the coins with the greater value first.

Variation

Have students do this activity using the dime and penny cut-outs and the play money on a small blank chart. Then have them pick up a few coins and see if they can count them without the help of the chart.

Use this opportunity to discuss fractional parts. Ask, "When using the dime cut-outs, how many equal parts did it take to cover the whole region?" (10) "A dime is one-tenth (1 out of 10 equal parts) of the whole dollar. What fractional part of the whole region do three dime cut-outs cover?" (³⁄₁₀) "How many penny cut-outs will cover a dime strip?" (10) "A penny is one-tenth of a dime. How many penny cut-outs did it take to cover the whole chart?" (100) "A penny is one one-hundredth of a dollar."

91. Fair Trade for a Dollar

Objective:	Practice with the value and name of the penny and dime
Grade level:	1–2
Group size:	Small group
Materials:	Top half of the dime and penny fair trade mats (page 106); play pennies, dimes, and dollar bills; and a die or dice
Procedure:	Players take turns rolling the die, collecting the number of pennies shown on the die, and placing the pennies on the mat under *PENNIES*. When a player has collected ten pennies, the player can trade them for a dime to place on the mat under *DIMES*. At the end of each player's turn, he or she should state the names of the coins and the total value. (For example, "I have three dimes and six pennies, 36 cents.") You may want to have students record the amounts on paper to practice writing the cent and dollar signs. To make the game move faster, have players roll several dice each turn. As the game progresses, students will learn it is quicker to get a dime and a penny when they roll 11 than it is to get eleven pennies and then make a trade for a dime. The first player who has ten dimes to trade for a dollar is the winner.

Variation

Each player begins with a dollar and gives away the amount they roll on the die or dice. The first person to give away the whole dollar is the winner. Note that players will need to trade the dollar bill for ten dimes right away. After players have made the trade, ask them if they still have a dollar on their mat. Be sure they understand a dollar bill has the same value as ten dimes or nine dimes and ten pennies. When students know they still have a dollar after these trades, they are ready to give away some pennies. At the end of each player's turn, he or she should state the total value still showing on the mat.

92. Counting Dimes and Pennies

Objective: Counting dimes and pennies

Grade level: 1–2

Group size: Individuals

Materials: Money cards (see page 10) and small numeral charts (page 91) for reference

Procedure: Use the money cards at a learning center to help students practice counting dimes and pennies, writing each amount, and ordering the amounts from least to greatest. You may also want to show students how to write amounts less than a dollar using a dollar sign. Discuss the fractional part of a whole dollar $0.34 represents. Students can use the small numeral chart to help them count or understand fractional parts in relation to the whole. The cards are self-corrective with the answers on the back.

93. Trade for Dimes

Objective: Practice with the value of pennies and dimes

Grade level: 1–2

Group size: Small group

Materials: Using head and tail stamps, stamp 20 cards with a dime and 36 cards with from 1 to 9 pennies (each amount four times)

Procedure: Choose one student to be the leader. The leader begins by slowly turning over one penny card at a time. Whenever any player sees a combination that makes a dime, he or she says, "dime," collects those penny cards, and trades them for a dime card from the leader. Then the leader continues to turn over penny cards for the players to claim and trade for a dime card. The player with the most dime cards is the winner.

Variation 1
Use the cards at a learning center for individual students to match sets of penny cards to a dime card. They do not have to use all the cards. Students can have a friend check their matching.

Variation 2
Use all the penny cards and eighteen dime cards for a problem-solving activity. Ask students to match the dime cards to sets of penny cards so *no* cards are left. Yes, it is possible!

94. Fair Trade for Ten Dollars

Objective: Practice with the value of pennies, dimes, and dollars

Grade level: 2–3

Group size: Small group

Materials: Bottom half of the dime and penny fair trade mats (page 106), blue game markers for pennies, red game markers for dimes, and green game markers for dollars

Procedure: This activity is just like Activity 91, except students trade for $10, and use chips for trading. Students will need to remember that it takes ten blues to trade for a red, and it takes ten reds to trade for a green. At the end of each player's turn, he or she should tell how much is still showing on his or her mat in terms of the coins and the value. Then the player should record the amount on paper.

95. Nickel's Worth

Objective: Practice with the value and name of the nickel

Grade level: 1–2

Group size: Whole class

Materials: Small pictorial charts (pages 89–90), nickel cut-outs (page 117), and play nickels; and for the variation, small numeral and blank charts (pages 91–92)

Procedure: Have students use small pictorial charts to work on nickels and counting by fives. Ask, "How many spaces does a nickel cut-out cover on the chart?" (5) "A nickel is worth five cents." "How many nickel cut-outs does it take to cover what a dime covers?" (2) Then ask students to find out how many nickel cut-outs it takes to cover 55, 35, 70, the whole chart, and so on. Most students will need to actually place the cut-outs on the chart to find the answers. After spending time having students count by fives, have them use play money in the same manner on their pictorial charts. They should place each nickel where the nickel cut-out strip ended (5, 10, 15, 20 … 100). The pictorial chart is a good visual aid for having students practice starting at any given multiple of 5 and counting on by fives.

Variation
Have students do this activity using the nickel cut-outs and play money on small numeral blank charts. Then have them pick up a few nickels and see if they can count them without the help of the charts.

Discuss fractional parts as the equal parts of a region. Since it takes 20 nickel cut-outs to cover the whole chart, each cut-out covers $\frac{1}{20}$ of the whole. If the dime strip is the whole and it takes 2 nickel cut-outs to cover one dime strip, a nickel is $\frac{1}{2}$ of the dime. If the nickel strip is the whole and it takes 5 equal penny cut-outs to cover the nickel strip, then a penny is $\frac{1}{5}$ of a nickel.

96. More Fair Trade

Objective: Practice with the value of dimes, nickels, and pennies

Grade level: 1–2

Group size: Small group

Materials: Small numeral charts (page 91), a money spinner with 1¢, 5¢, and 10¢ (page 113), dime, nickel, and penny cut-outs (page 117); for Variation 1, play dimes, nickels, and pennies and small blank charts (page 92); and for Variation 2, the dime, nickel, and penny fair trade mats (page 107)

Procedure: Players take turns spinning the spinner, collecting the amount they spin, and placing the cut-outs on the numeral chart. Players must make a trade when possible, so the smallest number of cut-outs is on the chart at one time. Players should place the cut-outs with the greatest value at the top of the chart so that counting them first becomes natural. After each player's turn, the player tells how much he or she has by coin names and by counting the total value. (For example, "I have three dimes, one nickel, and four pennies; a total of 10, 20, 30, 35, 36, 37, 38, 39 cents.") Players can use the chart to help them count the total. The first player to have ten dime cut-outs is the winner.

Variation 1
Have students play this game using the dimes, nickels, and pennies in play money. Then have them play with cut-outs and play money on a blank chart. Students should be able to count a handful of dimes, nickels, and pennies without the help of the charts.

Variation 2
Play "Fair Trade for a Dollar" (see Activity 91 for procedure), this time adding nickels and using the dime, nickel, and penny fair trade mats. Use play money and either a regular die or the money spinner with 1¢, 5¢, and 10¢ to play the game. Players take turns collecting and trading coins; five pennies are traded for a nickel, two nickels for a dime, and ten dimes for a dollar. When each player has traded for the dollar, then reverse the game; players now give away the amount rolled. The first player who trades back to an empty mat is the winner.

97. Cover Your Chart

Objective:	Counting with dimes, nickels, and pennies
Grade level:	1–2
Group size:	Whole class
Materials:	Small numeral charts (page 91); play dimes, nickels, and pennies; and money cut-outs (page 117) available at a learning center
Procedure:	In this activity students use the play money on the numeral chart (unless they still need to go back and use the cut-outs) to practice counting dimes, nickels, and pennies. Call out the coins to be placed on the chart and counted. For example:

- 3 dimes, 3 nickels, 3 pennies
- 1 dime, 6 nickels, 2 pennies
- 4 dimes, 1 nickel, 4 pennies
- 7 dimes, 7 pennies
- 8 nickels, 6 pennies

Gradually have students count coins mentally—just looking at the chart. Then have them count coins without a chart. Give students a handful of dimes, nickels, and pennies for them to count for you as a final check of their understanding.

98. "Seeing Money"

Objective:	Counting dimes, nickels, and pennies
Grade level:	1–3
Group size:	Whole class
Materials:	Pictorial cards made from the large chart (see page 6) and play dimes, nickels, and pennies; and for the variation, large pictorial chart and catcher's mitt (see page 7)

Procedure: Give each student about four cards and some play money. Tell students to count out play money to match the cards. Explain that the cards show "dimes" and that the ones are arranged to be groups of a "nickel" plus some "pennies." For example: 42 is 4 dimes and 2 pennies; 87 is 8 dimes, 1 nickel, and 2 pennies. Partners can read each of their cards to each other and then count the amount aloud.

Variation (Active)
Post a large pictorial chart where students can see it. Ask a student to use a pointer or the catcher's mitt to "catch" money numbers that you "throw." For example, when you say, "Point to 8 dimes, 1 nickel, 3 pennies," the student should point to the square that shows 88.

99. Stamp a Money Chart (Active)

Objective: Counting with dimes, nickels, and pennies

Grade level: 1–3

Group size: Small group

Materials: Large 1 to 100 blank chart made on butcher paper and dime, nickel, and penny coin stamps (heads and tails)

Procedure: Have two students work together to stamp a row of the money chart. The first student should stamp a penny in the first square, the other student should stamp two pennies in the next square. The two students should keep alternating in this way, always using the fewest coin stamps possible to represent each number in dimes, a nickel, and some pennies. Have the large pictorial chart available for reference. Notice that some money amounts, those with fewer coins, are more easily recognized.

100. Money Quiz

Objective: Experience in problem solving

Grade level: 2–3

Group size: Whole class

Materials: Dimes, nickels, and pennies in play money and paper and pencil

Procedure: Ask students to think of as many ways as they can to make 15 cents using only dimes, nickels, and pennies. Then ask them to think of as many ways as they can to make 25 cents. List their random solutions on the chalkboard. Then help them make charts like the ones below to organize the data.

dimes	1	1					
nickels	1		3	2	1		
pennies		5		5	10	15	
total coins	2	6	3	7	11	15	

4   4 4 4

MAKING 15 CENTS

dimes	2	2	1	1	1						
nickels	1		3	2	1	5	4	3	2	1	
pennies		5		5	10		5	10	15	20	25
total coins	3	7	4	8	12	5	9	13	17	21	25

4   4 4   4 4 4 4 4

MAKING 25 CENTS

101. Money to Spend

Objective: Experience in problem solving

Grade level: 2–3

Group size: Whole class

Materials: Two dimes, two nickels, and two pennies in play money and paper and pencil

Procedure: Start by saying, "You have two dimes, two nickels, and two pennies to spend. Number your paper from 1 to 32. Then cross out each amount you cannot spend using only those six coins." Allow plenty of time for students to figure it out for themselves. Ask, "Do you notice a pattern? Explain why it works." (Since there are only two pennies, it is only possible to make amounts that are two more than the multiples of 5 and 10. This means the numbers with 3, 4, 8, 9 in the ones place are always crossed out.)

1	2	3̶	4̶	5	6	7	8̶	9̶	10	11	12	1̶3̶	1̶4̶	15	16
17	1̶8̶	1̶9̶	20	21	22	2̶3̶	2̶4̶	25	26	27	2̶8̶	2̶9̶	30	31	32

102. Quarters/Half Dollars Worth

Objective: Practice with the value and name of the quarter and half dollar

Grade level: 1–2

Group size: Whole class

Materials: Small numeral charts (page 91), quarter and half dollar cut-outs (pages 115–116), play quarters and half dollars; and for the variation, small blank charts (page 92)

Procedure: Ask students how many spaces a quarter cut-out covers. Say, "A quarter is worth 25 cents." Then ask students to figure out how many quarter cut-outs it takes to cover the whole "dollar" chart, how many penny cut-outs it takes to cover a quarter cut-out, how many nickel cut-outs it takes to cover a quarter cut-out, how many dime and nickel cut-outs it takes to cover a quarter cut-out, two quarter cut-outs, three quarter cut-outs, and four quarter cut-outs. Then have students place four play money quarters on the 25, 50, 75, and 100 spaces on the chart. Do this until students can count by quarters easily. Then ask them how many quarters are in $1.75, $2.25, and so on. Help them think of each chart as a dollar bill. Then discuss the meaning of *a half*. Use the half dollar cut-out to see how many spaces it covers on the chart. Say, "A half dollar is worth 50 cents." Ask students what spaces on the chart to place the play money half dollars on.

Variation

Do this activity with the small blank charts. Watch to see that the students place the cut-outs and play money on the correct spaces. Have them try to count a few quarters and half dollars without the assistance of any chart.

Discuss fractional parts again. The money cut-outs make it easy to count and fit the fractional parts. A quarter is ¼ of the whole chart, a half dollar is ½ of the whole chart, a nickel is ⅕ of a quarter, a dime is ⅕ of a half dollar, a nickel is ⅒ of a half dollar, and so on.

103. Spin to Win

Objective: Practice with all coin values

Grade level: 2–3

Group size: Small group

Materials: Money mats (page 108), one of the money spinners on page 114, money cut-outs (pages 115–117), and play money

Procedure: Players take turns spinning either spinner, collecting the amount spun in either play money or cut-outs, and placing it on the mat in the correct space. Players should always make trades so that the fewest possible coins are on the mat at one time. Each player counts the money aloud at the end of his or her turn. Encourage students to count the money starting with the coin with the greatest value. At the end of each round, players compare their amounts. Players continue to spin, trade, and count until someone has one dollar. That player is the winner. Have numeral charts available if students need help in counting.

Variation

Each player begins with a dollar. Players take turns spinning, trading, and giving away play money until someone has no money left. That player is the winner. Or, have players spin, trade, and count five dollars. Then they can play by starting with five dollars and giving it away.

104. Cover and Count

Objective: Practice with all coin values

Grade level: 2–3

Group size: Small group

Materials: Small numeral charts (page 91) and play money; money cut-outs (pages 115–117) available for reference

Procedure: Dictate an amount of money to the group. Students should place play money on the correct spaces on their charts. Have the money cut-outs available for students to use for checking. Allow enough time for students to experiment with different possibilities. Then ask, "What coins did you use? Can you find another way? What is the fewest number of coins you can use?" As students take the coins off the chart, have them count the coins aloud. (Note: To count from 25 to 35 when using play money students can use a quarter and a dime, but when using cut-outs, they will need to use two nickel cut-outs to place on the chart.) Then have students get certain coins that you tell them from the bank. For example, "Get a quarter, three dimes, one nickel, and two pennies." Ask, "How much is it?" (62¢) Allow students to use the numeral chart to count the money, but gradually encourage them not to use the chart and to do mental addition. Encourage them to count the coin with the greatest value first. Take plenty of time with this activity.

105. Money Walk (Active)

Objective: Practice with all coin values; using auditory and visual memory

Grade level: 2–3

Group size: Whole class

Materials: Giant 1 to 100 chart (see page 10) and small numeral charts (page 91)

Procedure: Place the giant chart in the middle of the floor or in the gym. Have students sit around the edge with their small numeral charts. While students take turns walking on the chart, the other children will "walk" with their fingers on their individual charts. Say, for example, "You have 23 cents. Walk on the coins you have in your pocket." The student may step on 10 and say "dime"; step on 20 and say "dime"; step on 21 and say "penny"; step on 22 and say "penny"; and then step on 23 and say "penny." Ask if someone can do it with other coins. Then ask, "Is there still another way?"

Variation 1
Call out a sequence with two to four coins and have a student walk that sequence on the giant chart, using either the numeral or blank side. For example, if you say, "quarter, dime, penny," the student should walk on 25, 35, 36.

Variation 2
Have sequences of coins written on cards. Allow students time to study a card and then take it away. See if someone can walk that sequence.

Variation 3
Try mixing the sequence by not always saying the coin with the greatest value first. For example, if you say, "nickel, dime, nickel," the student should walk on 5, 15, 20. This requires good listening and a real understanding of coin values.

106. Stamp Me

Objective: Practice with all coin values

Grade level: 2–3

Group size: Individuals

Materials: Head and tail coin stamps and scratch paper

Procedure: Have two students work together on this activity at a learning center. First have each student divide a paper into 2 to 4 sections, write a number from 1 to 100 in cent notation in each section, stamp that amount, and count it aloud to his or her partner. Then have each student divide another paper into four sections, write the same amount in each section, stamp the amount four different ways, and count each one aloud to his or her partner. Then have each student divide another paper into three sections and stamp an amount in the center section. Partners can exchange papers and stamp what comes before and what comes after that amount in the other two sections. Instruct students to write the amounts using cent notation at the bottom of each section.

107. Stamp a Money Chart

Objective: Practice with all coin values and using cent notation

Grade level: 2–3

Group size: Small group

Materials: Large blank 1 to 100 chart drawn on butcher paper and head and tail money stamps; large numeral chart for reference and play money for checking

Procedure: The group will stamp a coin 1 to 100 chart and write the cent notation in the lower-right corner of each square. If necessary, students can use play money and a small numeral chart to help decide what is the fewest number of coins that can be put in each square. Encourage discussion. Students should take turns stamping a row and writing the amount for each square in the row. Do the children notice any coin patterns emerging? Talk about them. (Because students are to use the fewest coins possible, after they use a quarter for 25 cents, they will use a quarter and the same coins used for 1 to 24 to make the amounts 26 to 49. Then they will use a half dollar and the same coins for 51 to 74, and so forth.)

108.   How Many Coins?

Objective: Experience in problem solving

Grade level: 2–3

Group size: Small group or individuals

Materials: Play money and cards labeled as described below

Procedure: Have students draw a card and solve the problem by creating the amount on the card with exactly the given number of coins. Check their solutions, or have partners check on each other. You could make the cards self-corrective by writing the answers on the back. Here are a few suggested cards:

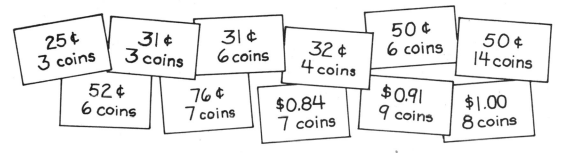

109.   Change to a Dollar

Objective: Experience in making change to a dollar and story problems

Grade level: 3–4

Group size: Whole class or small group

Materials: Small numeral charts (page 91), money cut-outs (pages 115–117), and play money

Procedure: Give a story problem in which the solution requires students to determine change to a dollar. For example, "You have a dollar and are going to the store. You buy some gum for 23 cents. What is your change?" There are several ways students can use the numeral chart to arrive at the answer. Some students will work back from 100, covering the last two rows and three spaces with money cut-outs to show that part of the dollar was used to buy the gum. This is a good method that provides answers quickly. Other students will use money cut-outs, starting at 24, to cover the rest of the chart and then count the change. This is a wonderful method for practicing counting on to give change for a dollar. Encourage students to use both methods. Be sure they understand the difference between giving an answer to a story problem and counting back the change for a partner. This activity should help students learn to make mental change quickly, to count back change as a clerk does, and to be able to verify that they have gotten the correct change when they are shopping. As you make up more story problems, you may want to have students start with 50¢, 80¢, $2.00, and so on. Students can use the same methods to arrive at the answers by using play money on the chart, just looking at the chart, and eventually without using a chart at all. By this time, students should have the "chart picture" in their minds as a referent for making change to a dollar.

110. Money Toss (Active)

Objective:	Practice in column addition, estimation, subtraction with regrouping, and dollar notation
Grade level:	3–4
Group size:	Small group
Materials:	Large numeral chart, five pennies for tossing, calculator, and paper and pencil
Procedure:	Place the chart on the floor and have the players gather around it. Each player tosses a penny onto the chart. Each player records all the numbers in a column, using the dollar sign and decimal point. Then each player records an estimate of the sum and then adds the amounts. For each round, one player checks the answer with a calculator. Each player who has the correct answer written with correct notation gets a point. The first player to get ten points is the winner.

Variation

Each player begins with ten dollars. Players take turns tossing a penny onto the chart to buy an item that costs the amount the penny lands on. After each player has bought five items, ask, "Who has the most change left? Who has the least change left?" Before the game begins, each player might like to estimate how much they will have after they buy five items.

Reproducible Pages

CHARTS AND GRIDS

Pictorial Chart (with flaps)   89
Pictorial Chart (without flaps)   90
Numeral Chart   91
Blank Chart   92
3 × 3 and 5 × 2 Grids   93

CARDS

Regular Domino Flash Cards   94
Modified Domino Flash Cards (dots)   95
Modified Domino Flash Cards (beans)   96
Ten-Frame Flash Cards   97
Pictorial Chart Flash Cards (ones)   98
Pictorial Chart Flash Cards (tens)   99
Expanded Notation Cards   100

SIGN CIRCLES

Large Sign Circles   101
Small Sign Circles   102

MATS

Place Value Mat   103
Tens and Ones Mat   104
Addition and Subtraction Mat   105
Fair Trade Mats (dime and penny)   106
Fair Trade Mats (dime, nickel, and penny)   107
Money Mat   108

SPINNERS

Pictorial Spinners   109
Tens and Ones Spinners   110
Expanded Notation Spinners   111
Word Name Spinners   112
More or Less Spinner, Money Spinners   113
Money Spinners   114

MONEY CUT-OUTS

Half Dollar Cut-Outs   115
Quarter Cut-Outs   116
Penny, Nickel, and Dime Cut-Outs   117

WORKSHEETS

Fill in the Blanks (pictorial)   118
Fill in the Blanks (numeral)   119
Pictorial Chart Segments   120
Pictorial Chart Segments   121
Numeral Chart Segments   122
Numeral Chart Segments   123
Tens and Ones Review   124
Tens and Ones Review   125
Tens and Ones Review   126
Complete the Patterns   127

TO CHART

TO ◇ CHART

1	2	3	4	5	6	7	8	9	10
11	12	13	14	15	16	17	18	19	20
21	22	23	24	25	26	27	28	29	30
31	32	33	34	35	36	37	38	39	40
41	42	43	44	45	46	47	48	49	50
51	52	53	54	55	56	57	58	59	60
61	62	63	64	65	66	67	68	69	70
71	72	73	74	75	76	77	78	79	80
81	82	83	84	85	86	87	88	89	90
91	92	93	94	95	96	97	98	99	100

1 TO 100 CHART

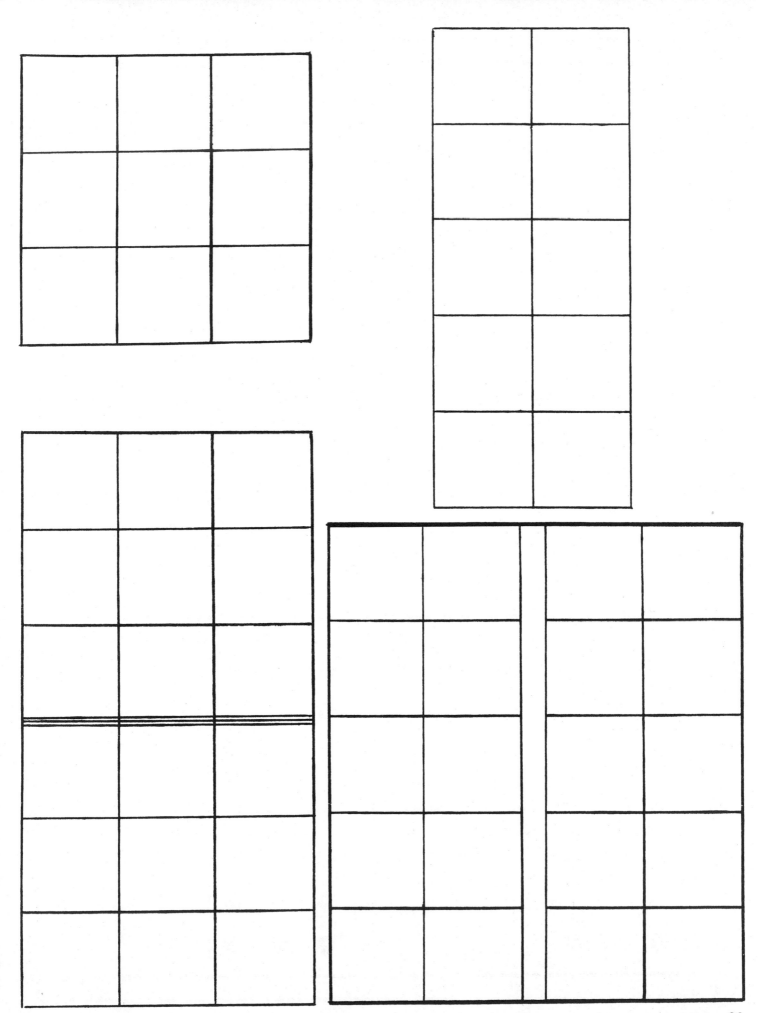

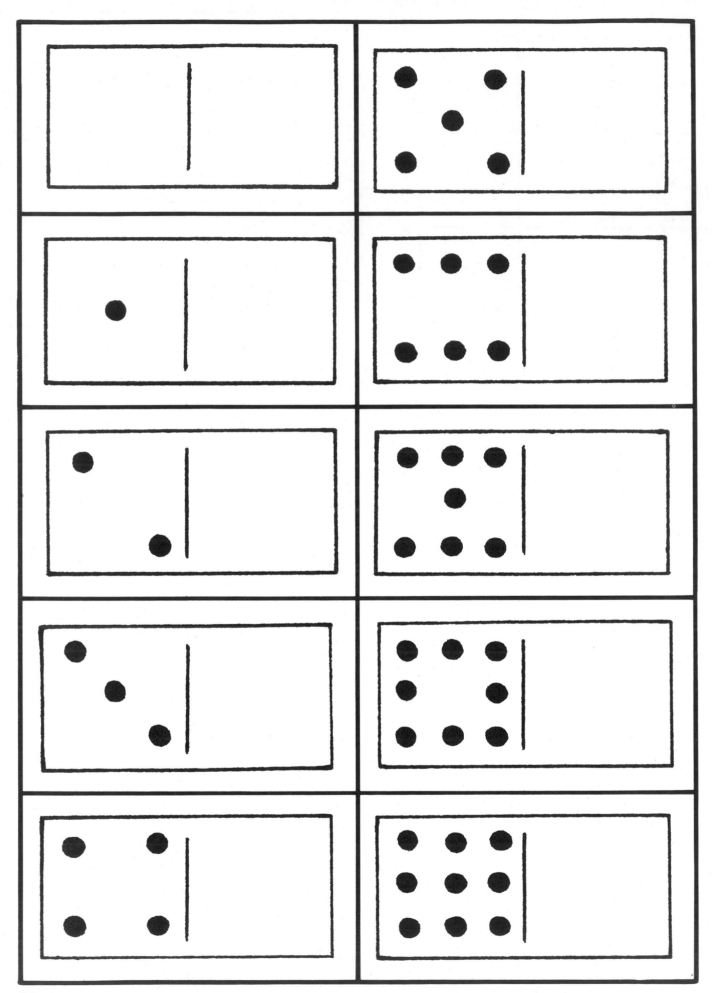

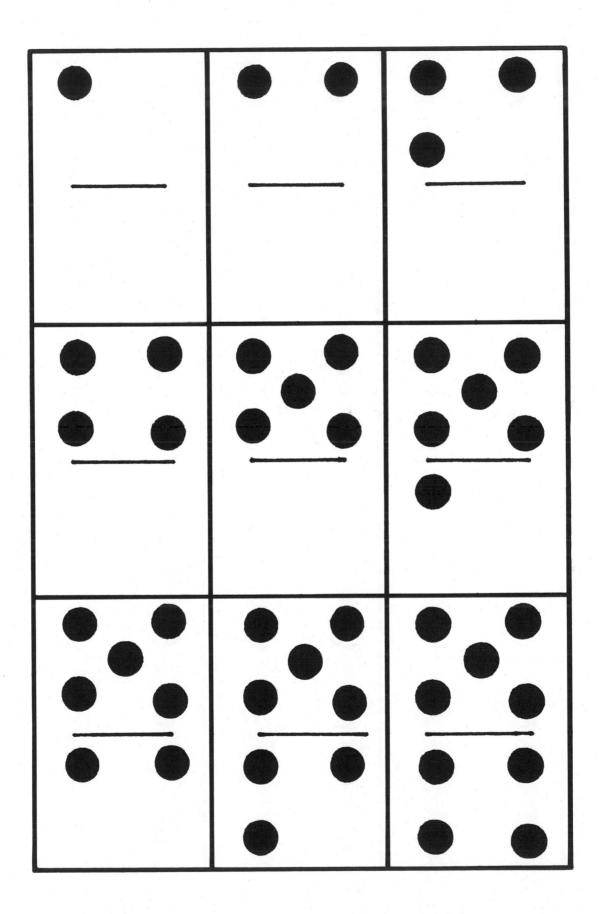

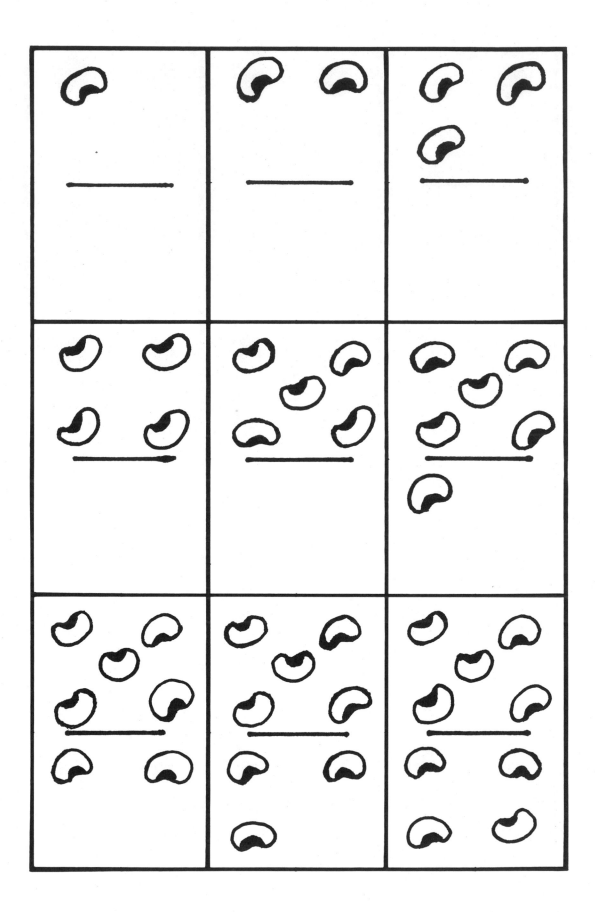

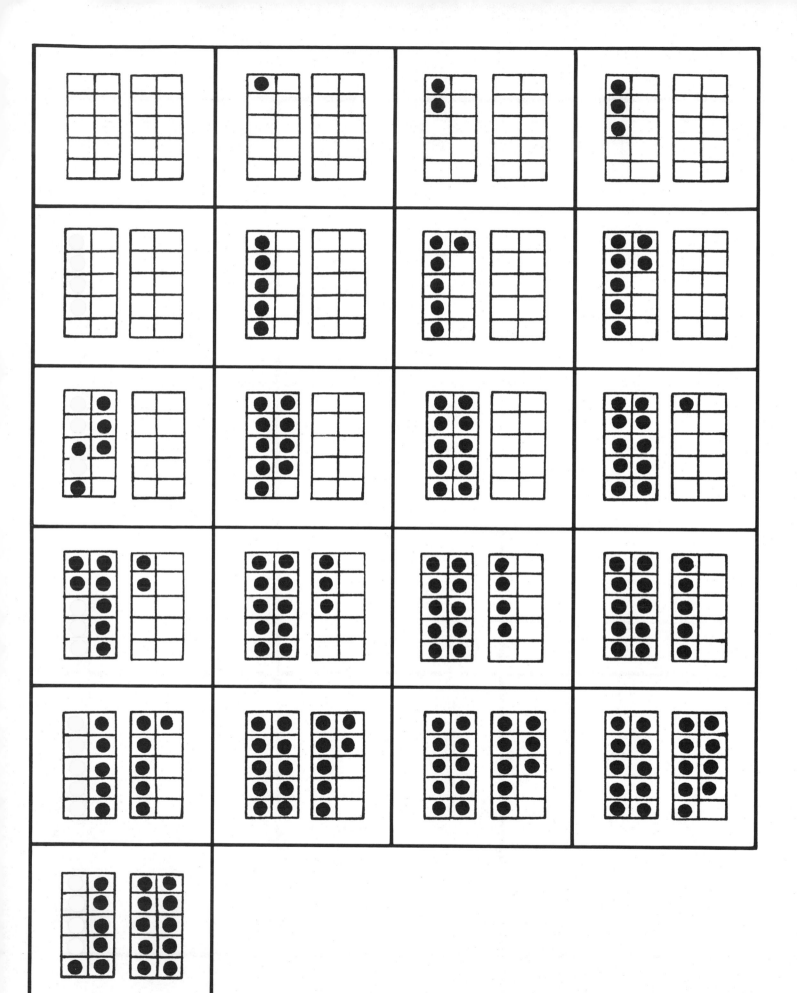

TEN-FRAME FLASH CARDS 97

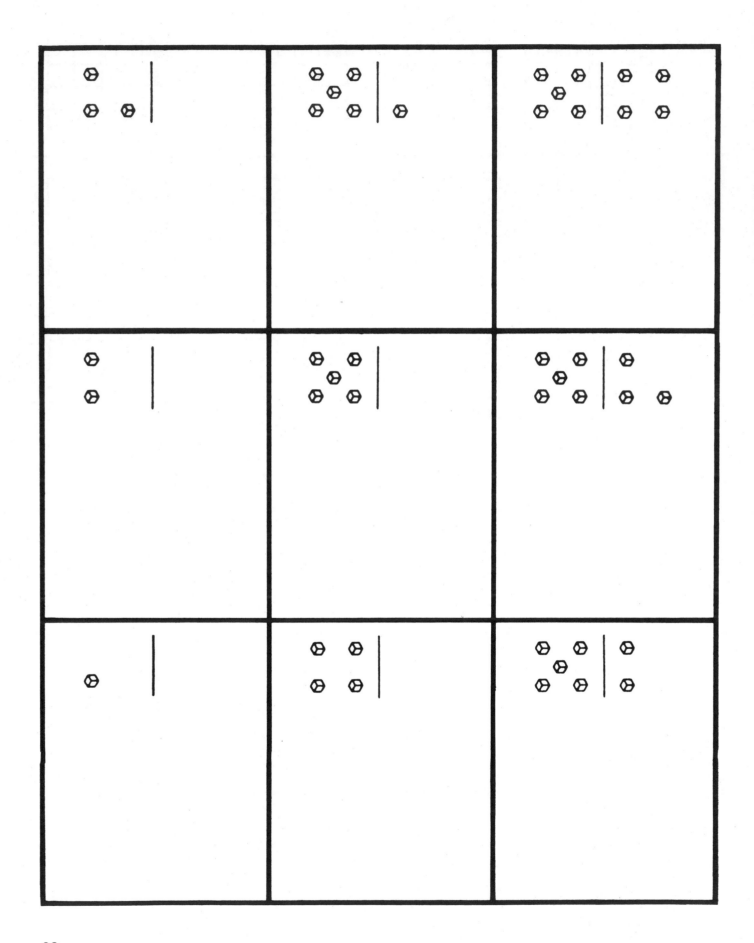

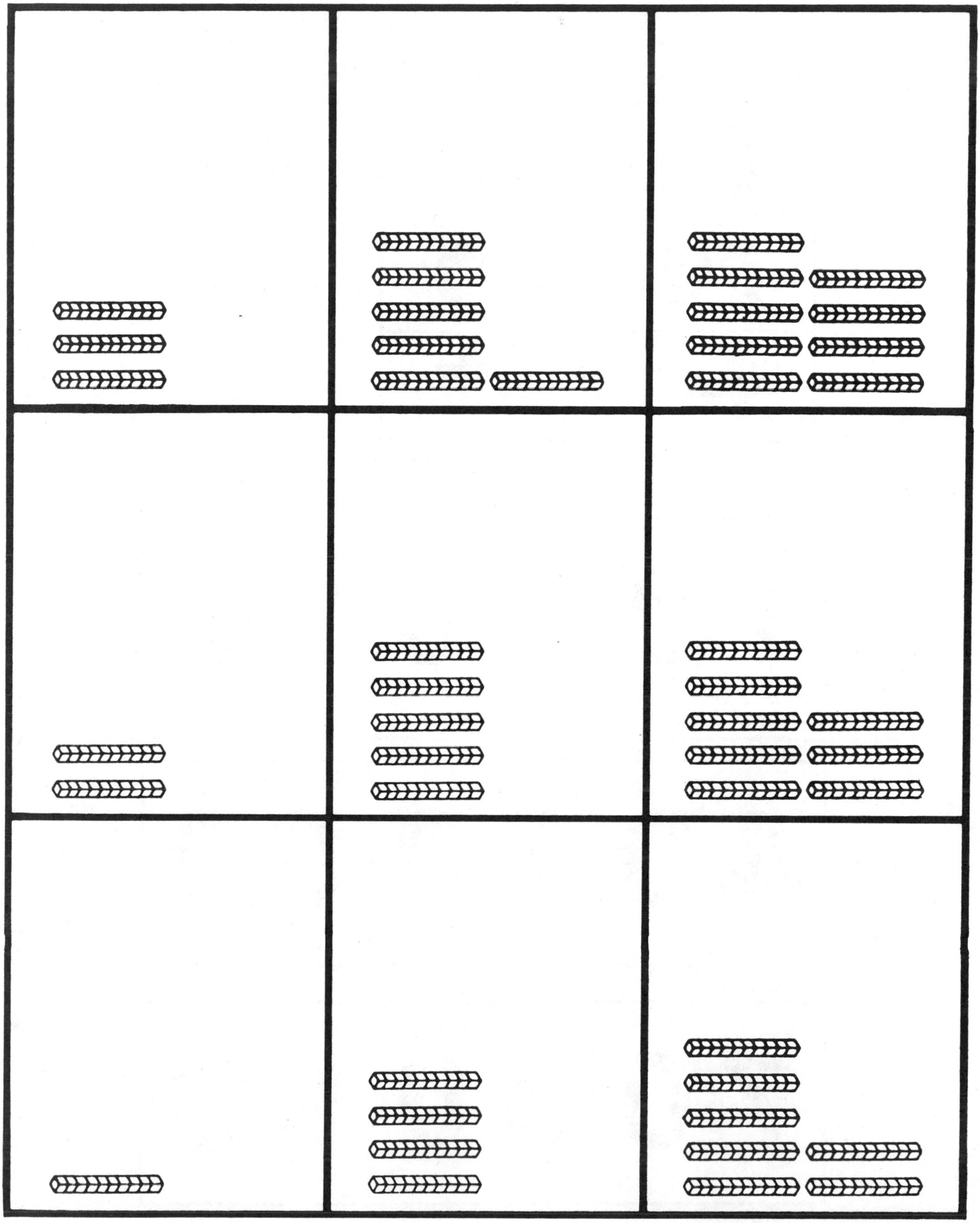

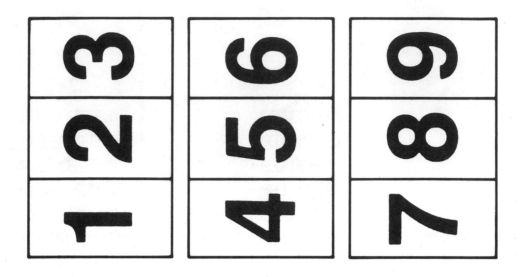

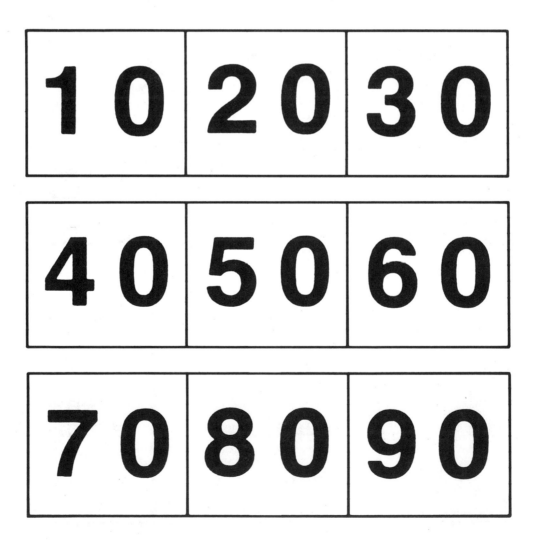

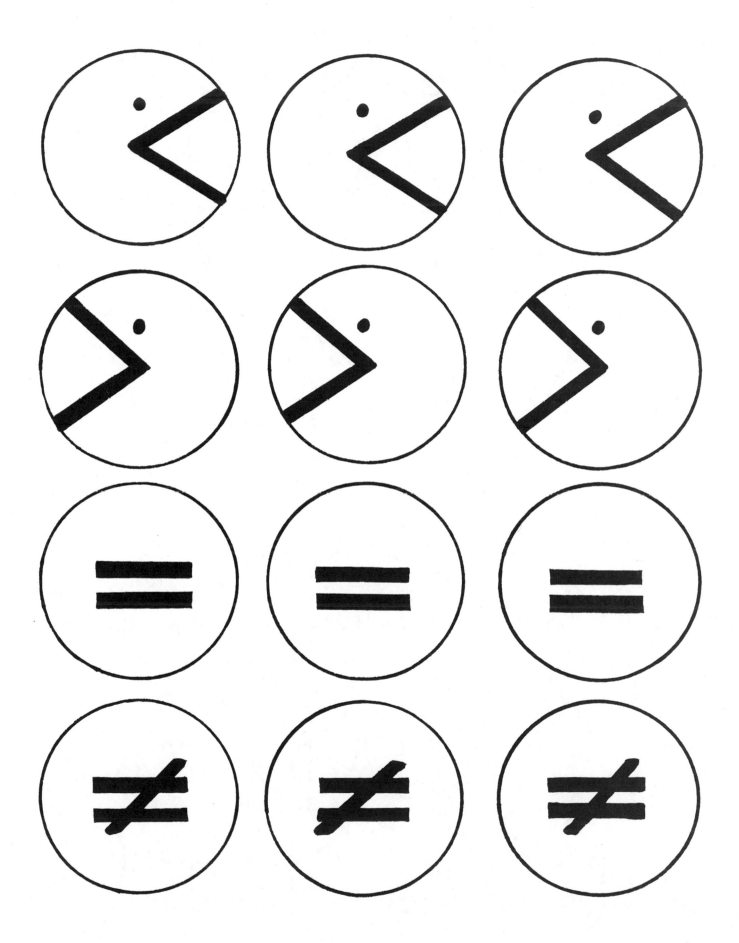

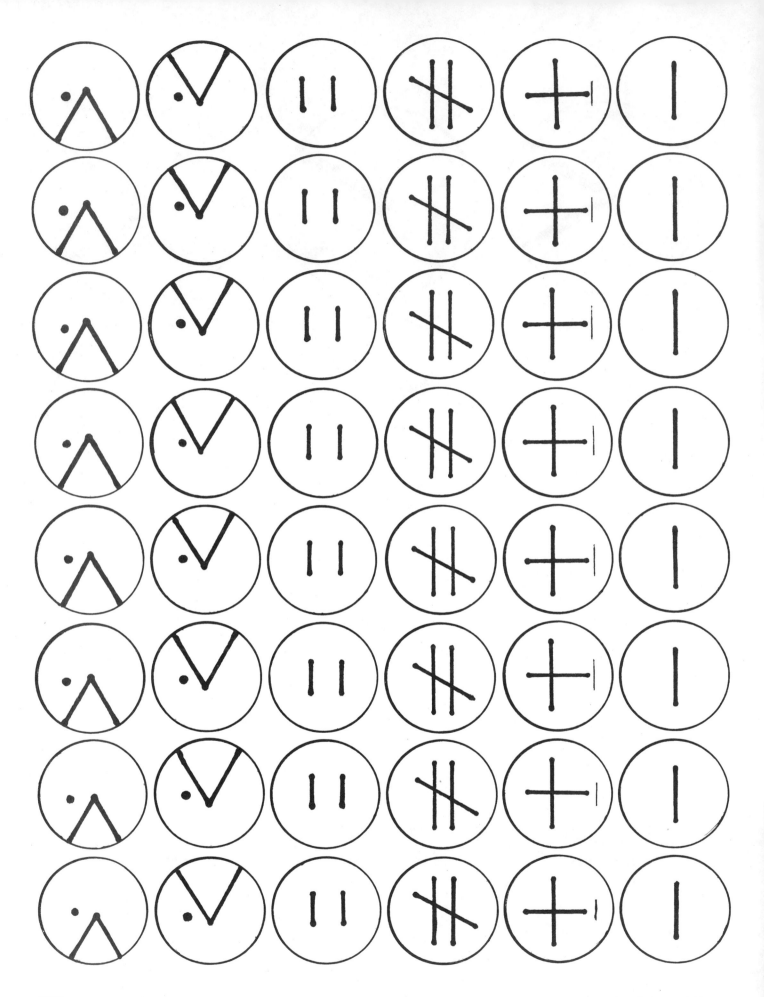

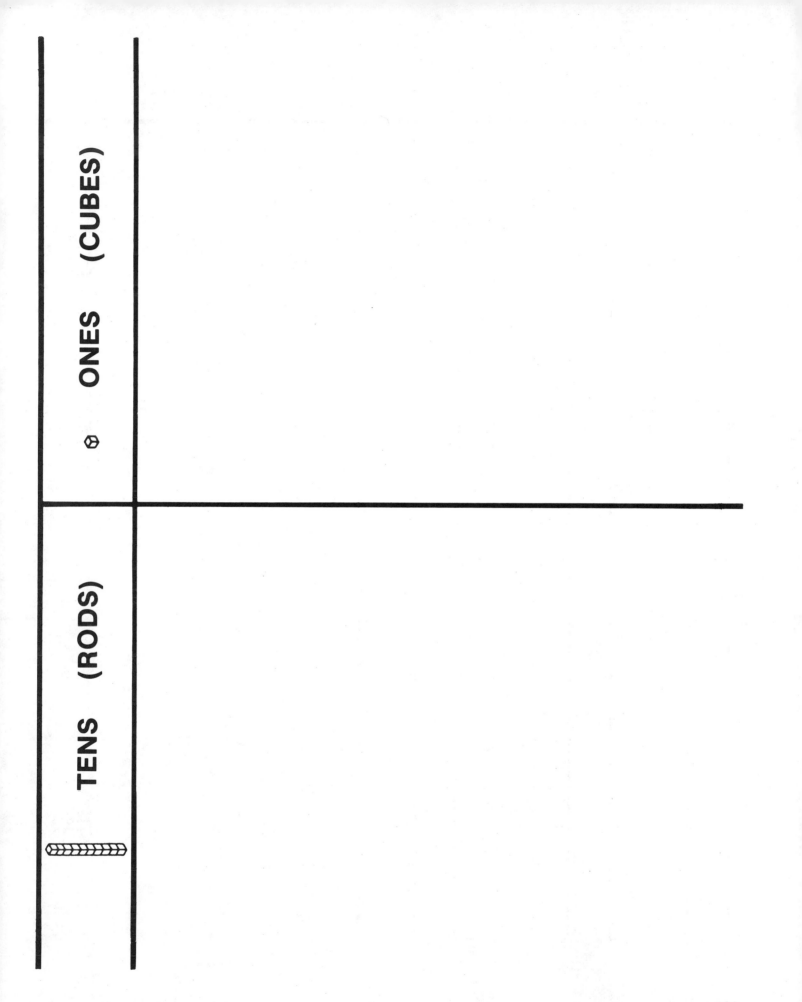

ONES (CUBES)

TENS (RODS)

TENS | ONES

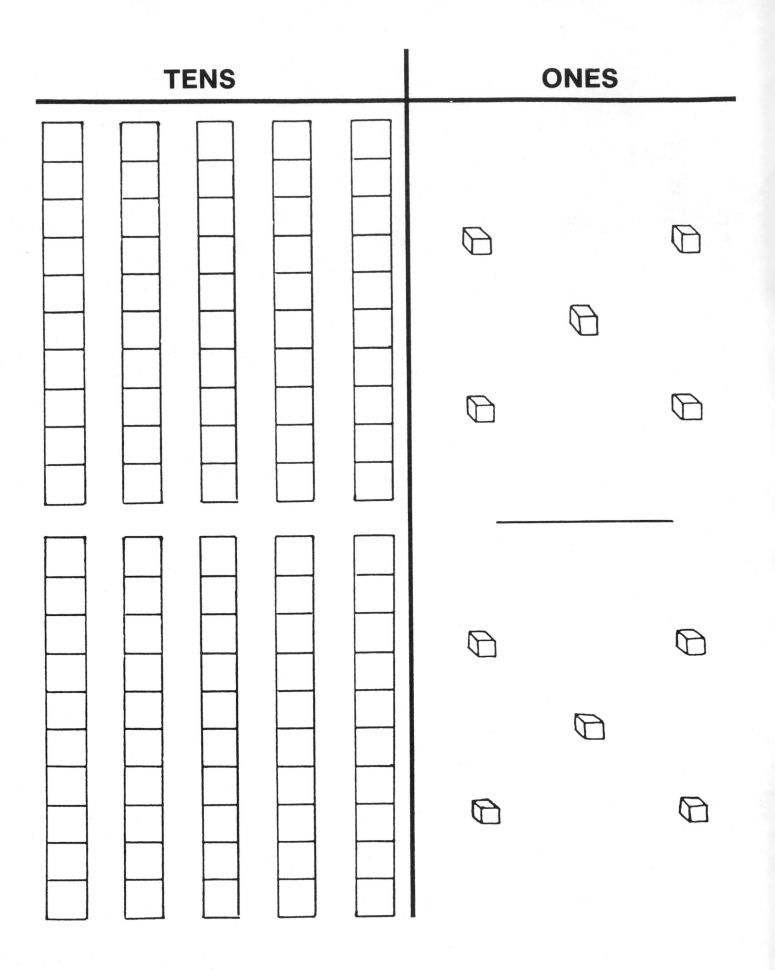

TENS   (RODS) | ONES   (CUBES)

DOLLAR HUNDRED 100	DIMES TENS 10	PENNIES ONES 1

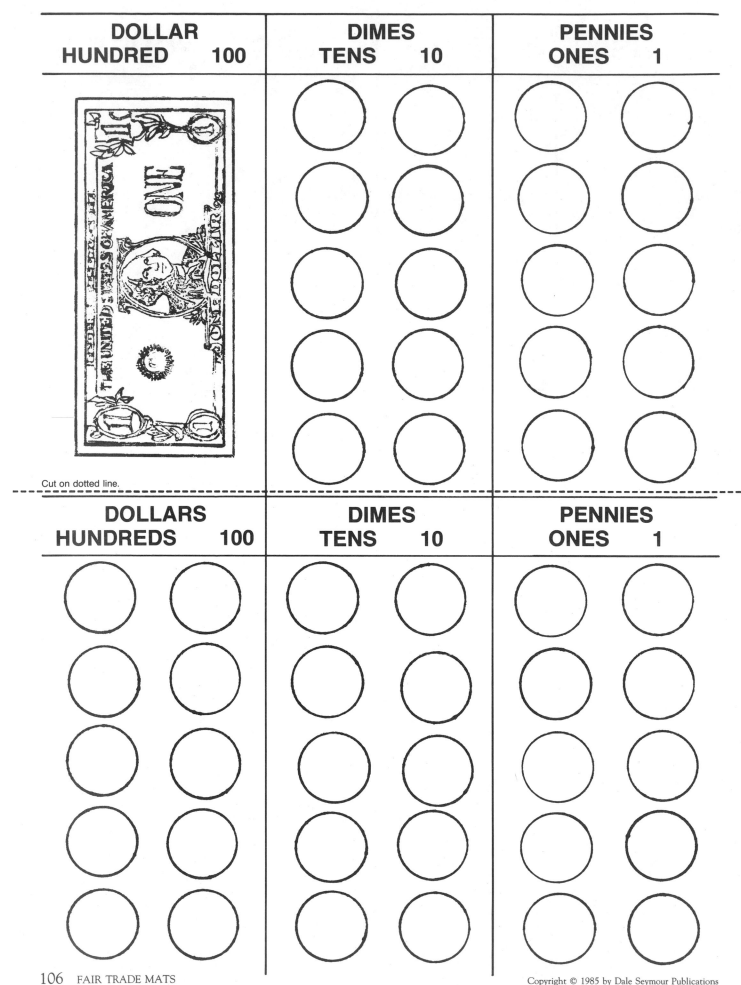

Cut on dotted line.

DOLLARS HUNDREDS 100	DIMES TENS 10	PENNIES ONES 1

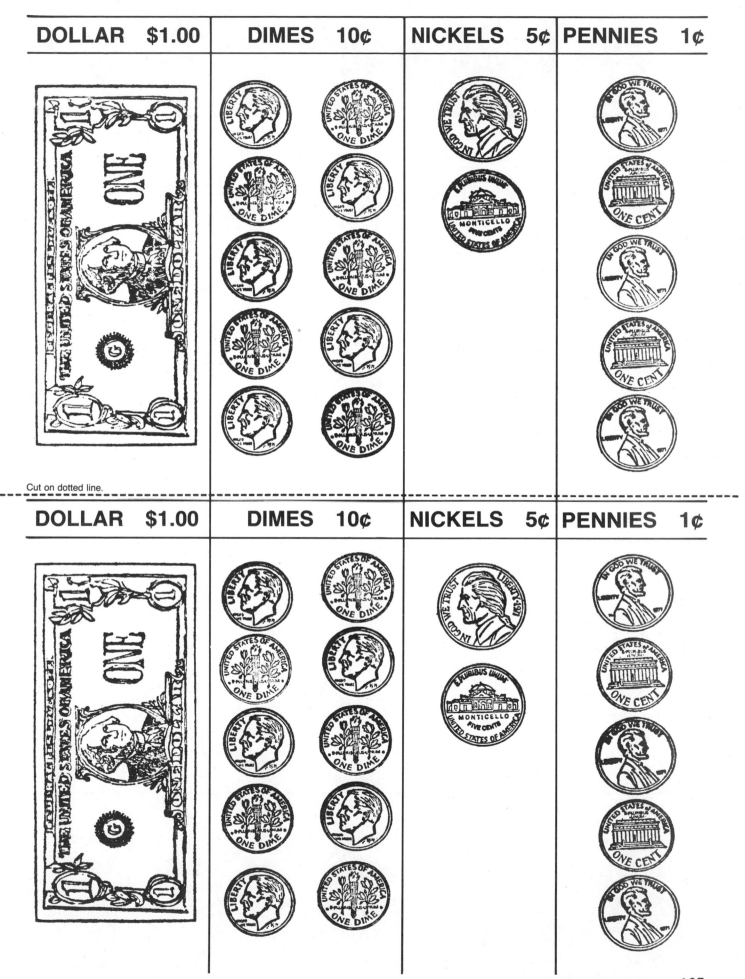

DOLLAR $1.00	DIMES 10¢	NICKELS 5¢	PENNIES 1¢

Cut on dotted line.

DOLLAR $1.00	DIMES 10¢	NICKELS 5¢	PENNIES 1¢

PENNIES 1¢	NICKELS 5¢	DIMES 10¢	QUARTERS 25¢	HALF DOLLARS 50¢	DOLLARS $1.00

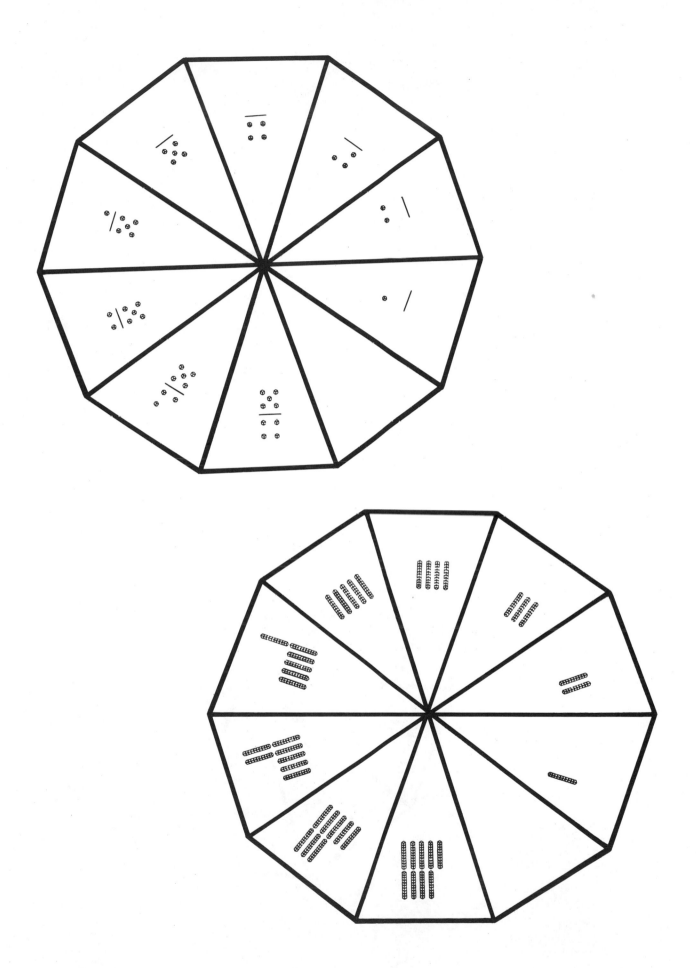

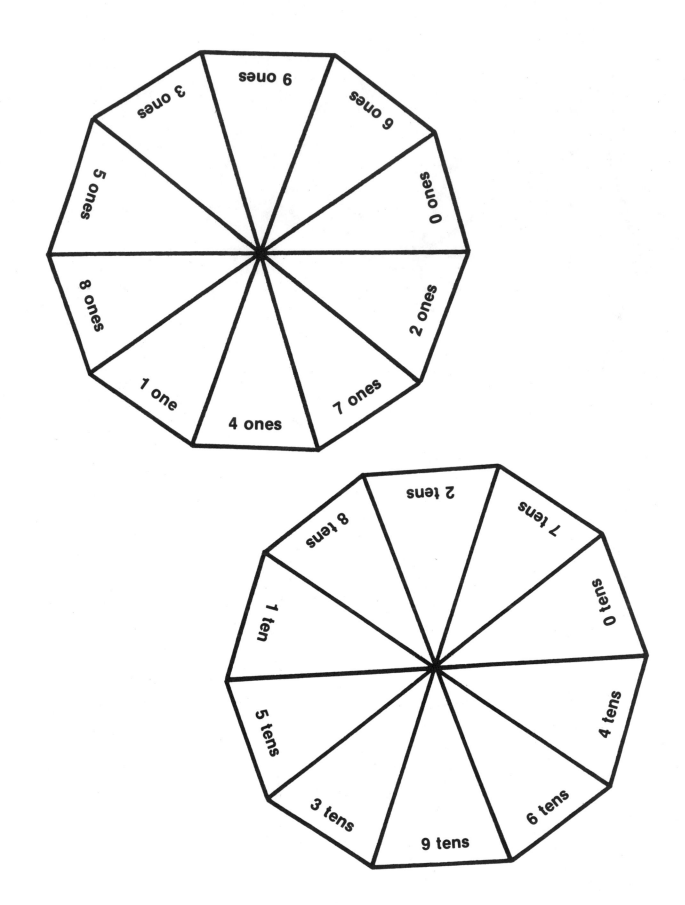

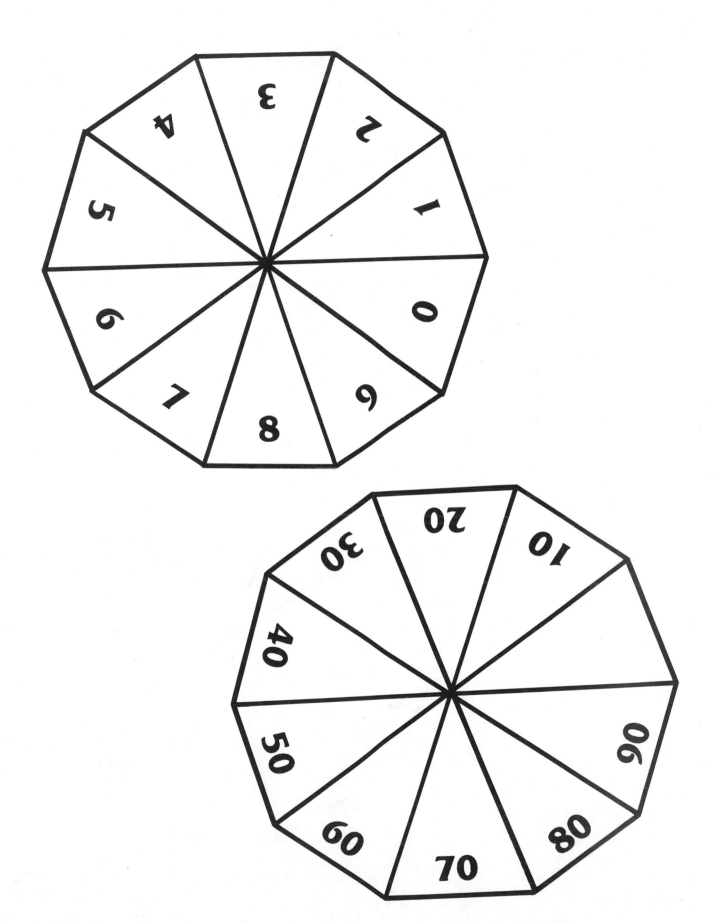

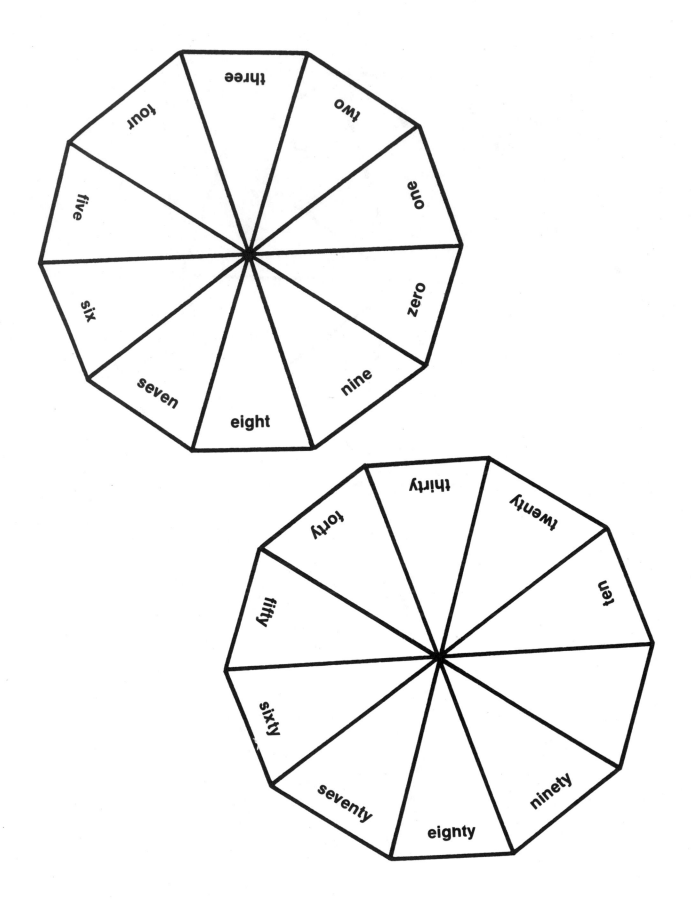

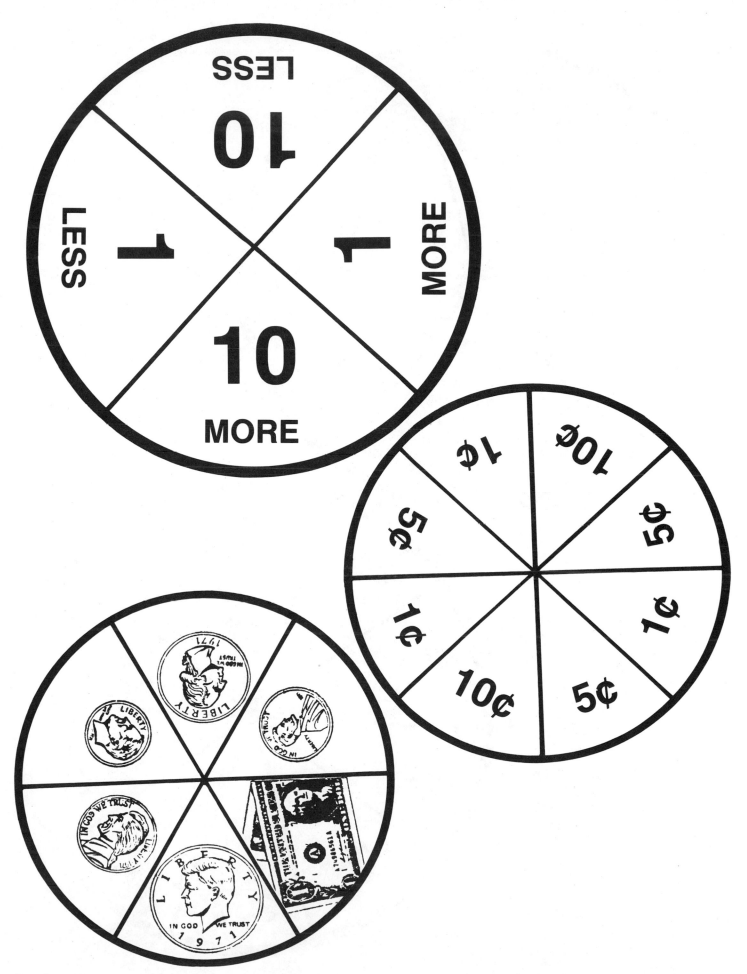

MORE OR LESS SPINNER, MONEY SPINNERS 113

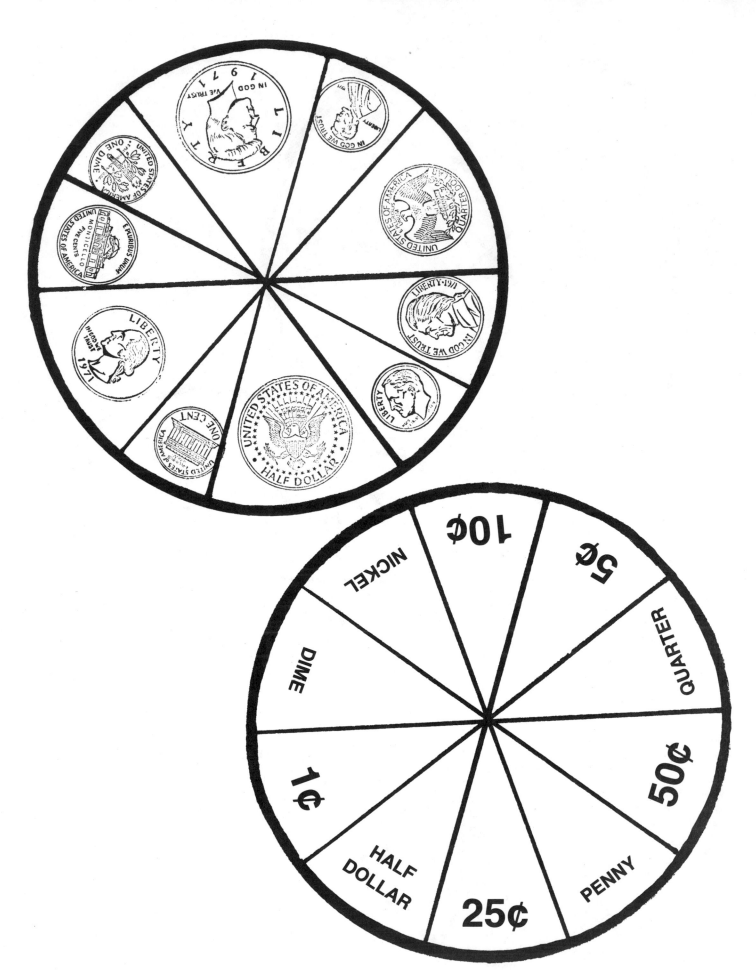

Cut around the outside and on the dotted line.

Cut around the outside and on the dotted lines.

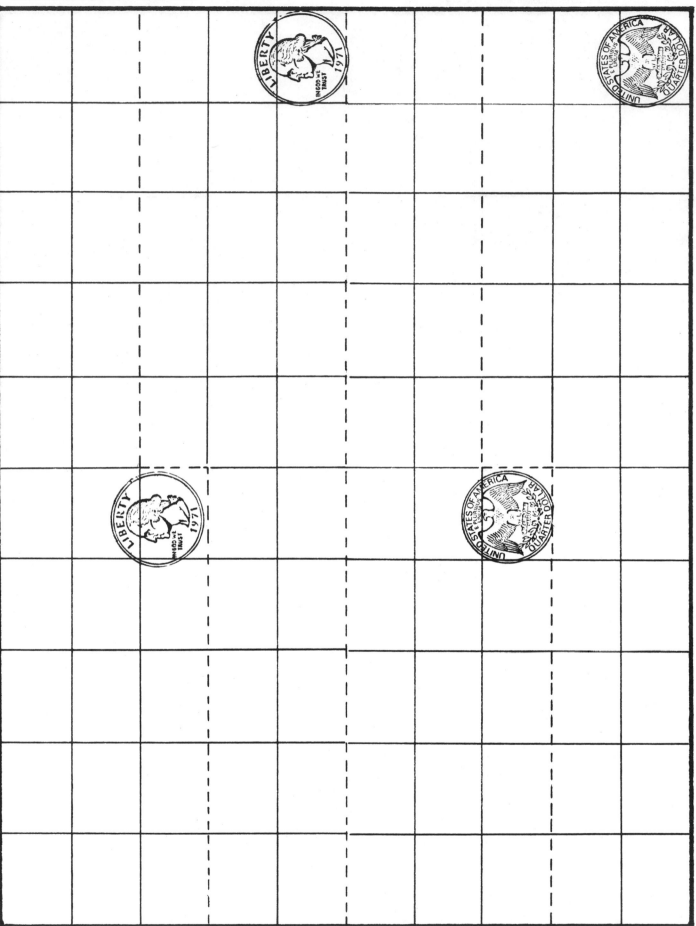

Cut around the outside and on the dotted lines.

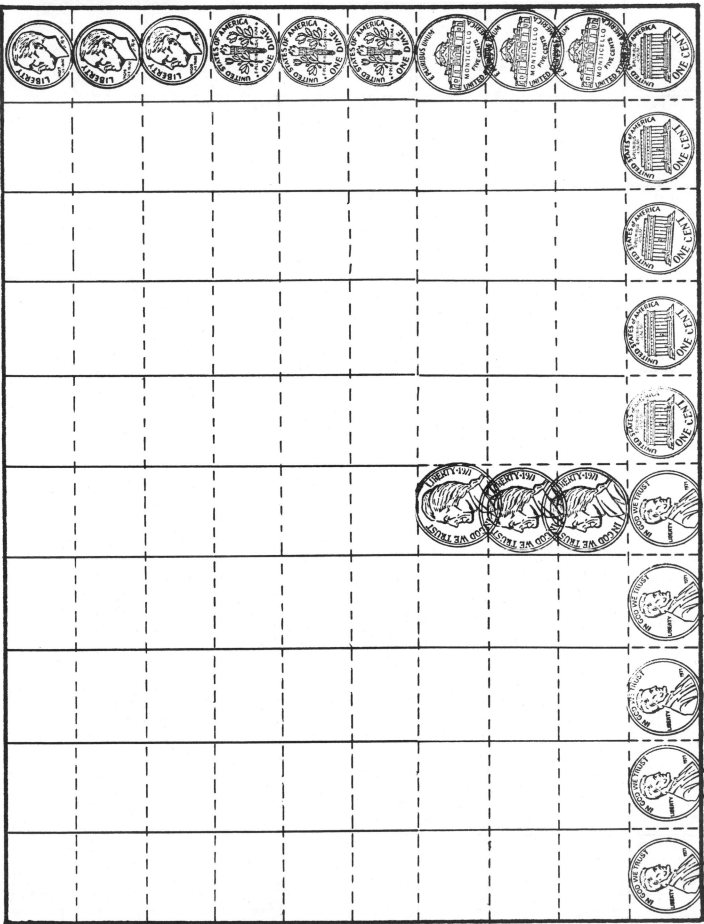

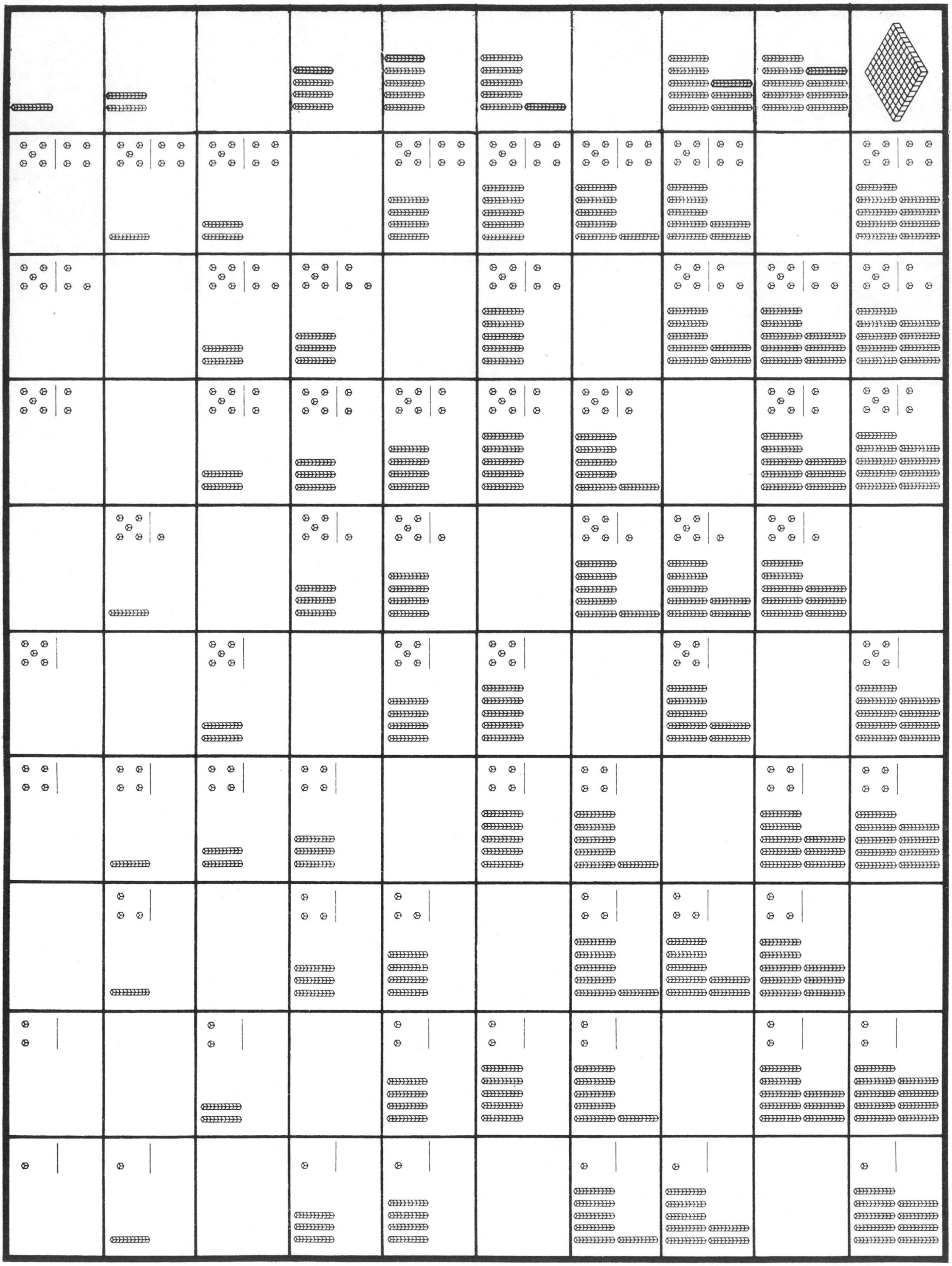

1	2		4	5			8	9	10
11			14		16	17			20
21		23		25	26		28	29	
	32			35		37		39	40
41	42		44		46	47		49	
		53	54	55		57	58		
61	62			65	66			69	70
	72		74		76	77	78		80
81		83		85	86			89	
91		93	94		96	97		99	100

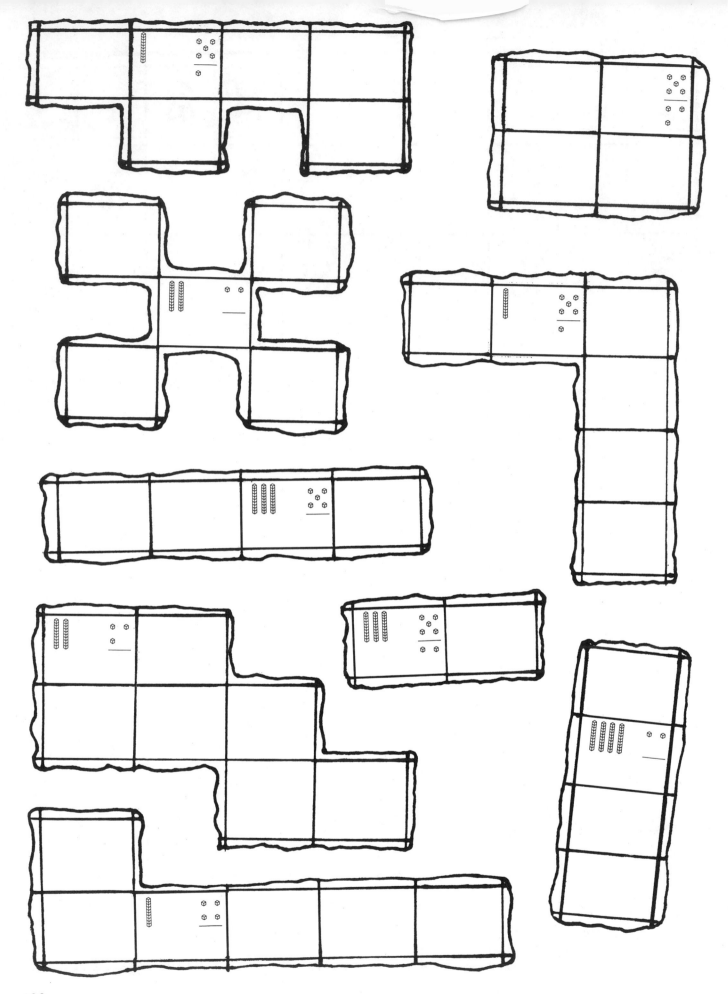

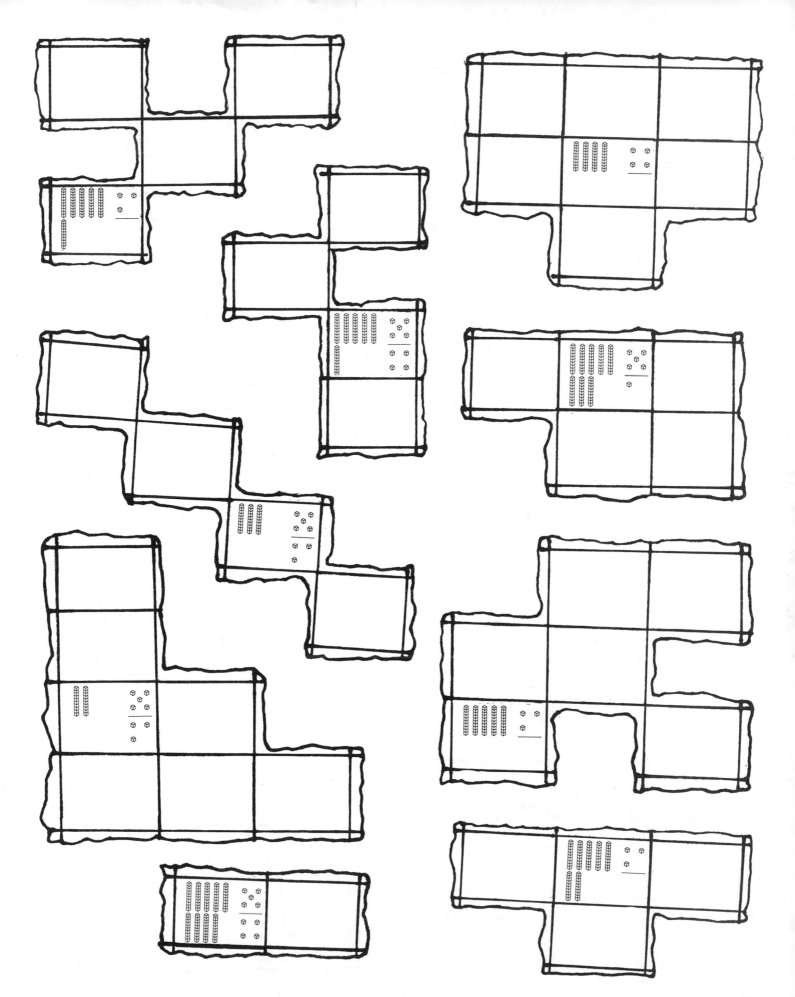

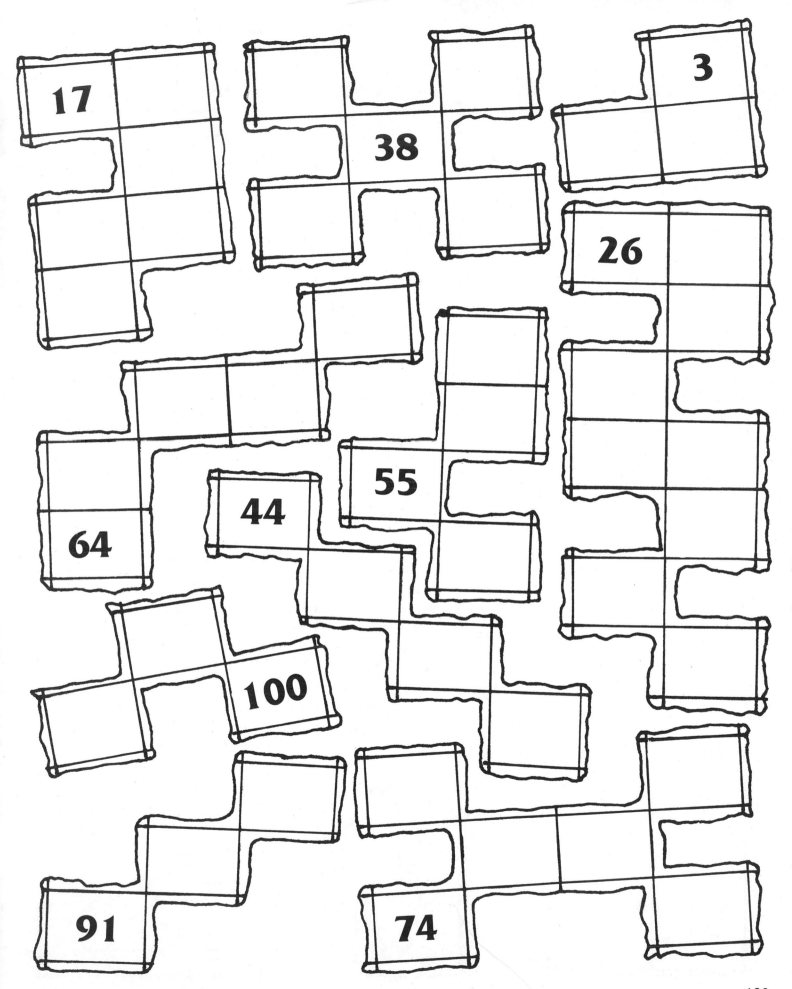

10 LESS	1 LESS	PICTURE AND NUMERAL	1 MORE	10 MORE
		25		
		77		
		34		
		40		
		29		
		62		

PICTURE	EXPANDED FORM	WORD FORM	NUMERAL
	20 + 4	2 tens + 4 ones	24
			81
	5 + 60		
		6 ones + 9 tens	
			19
		4 tens + 6 ones	
	70 + 2		

a. 3 tens and _____ ones = 37

b. _____ + 5 = 45

c. 70 + 8 = _____

d. 7 ones and 9 tens = _____

e. 20 + _____ = 21

f. _____ tens and 4 ones = 74

g. 33 = _____ + 3

h. 40 + _____ = 46

i. _____ ones and 6 tens = 64

j. 90 = 9 tens and _____ ones

k. 3 tens and _____ ones = 38

l. 1 ten and 9 ones = _____

m. 0 tens and 5 ones = _____

n. 40 + _____ = 43

o. _____ + 3 = 83

p. 49 = 9 ones and _____ tens

q. 80 = _____ tens and _____ ones

r. 49 = 9 ones and _____ tens

s. 80 = tens and _____ ones

t. 6 tens and _____ ones = 60

u. 50 + 2 = _____

v. 70 + _____ = 73

w. _____ + 5 = 65

x. 7 ones and 0 tens = _____

y. 43 = _____ tens and _____ ones

z. 9 tens and _____ ones = 93

Study the patterns and fill in the blanks.

a. 46, 47, ___, 49

b. 18, 16, 14, ___

c. 45, 35, ___, 15

d. 8, ___, ___, ___, 4, 3, 2, 1, 0

e. 1, 3, ___, 7, ___, ___, ___

f. 0, 2, 4, ___, ___, 10, 12

g. 19, 20, 29, 30, ___, ___, ___, 50

h. ___, 10, 15, 20, ___, ___, ___

i. ___, 54, ___, ___, 51, 50, 49

j. 10, ___, ___, ___, 50, 60, ___

k. 3, 6, 9, ___, 15, ___, ___

l. 69, 71, 73, ___, ___, ___, 81, 83

m. 70, 72, 74, ___, ___, ___, 82, ___

n. 7, 11, 15, 19, ___, ___, ___, ___

o. ___, ___, 14, 13, 12, ___, ___, ___

p. 65, 55, ___, ___, 25, ___

q. ___, 4, ___, 12, 16, 20, ___

r. ___, ___, ___, 58, 59, 60, ___

s. ___, ___, 18, ___, 22, 24, ___, ___

t. 0, 6, 12, 18, ___, ___, ___, 42

u. 19, 24, 29, ___, ___, ___, ___, ___, 59, 64

v. 91, 84, 77, ___, ___, ___, ___, 42, 35

w. 42, ___, ___, 51, ___, ___, 60, ___, ___, 69

x. 10, 19, 28, ___, ___, ___, 64, 73, ___